Covered Bridges

OF THE MIDDLE WEST

Former bridge over Mahoning River near Leavittsburg, Ohio.

Covered Bridges

OF THE

MIDDLE WEST

BY

RICHARD SANDERS ALLEN

BRATTLEBORO, VERMONT
The Stephen Greene Press
1970

TO MY SISTER
LUCY EMMA ALLEN
WHO BELIEVED AND ENCOURAGED

This book has been designed by R. L. Dothard Associates,
printed and bound by The Book Press and published by
The Stephen Greene Press, Brattleboro, Vermont 05301.

Library of Congress Catalog Card Number: 68-25812
International Standard Book Number: 0-8289-0105-8

ACKNOWLEDGMENTS

The research to complete this book was made possible only by a generous grant from the John Simon Guggenheim Memorial Foundation of New York, from whom the author received a 1962–63 Fellowship. I am in debt not only to the Foundation, but to those who had faith in my ability to carry out the project, and who said so.

A prime source of information was the archive material of various historical and engineering societies. This was obtained for the most part by personal perusal, with the aid of their fine and competent staffs. Among them were:

Baker Library, Harvard University, Boston
Engineering Societies Library, New York
Henry Ford Museum and Greenfield Village, Dearborn, Michigan
Indiana Historical Society, Indianapolis
Kansas State Historical Society, Topeka
Michigan Historical Commission, Lansing
Minnesota Historical Society, Saint Paul
Missouri Historical Society, Saint Louis
New-York Historical Society, New York
New York Public Library, New York
New York State Library, Albany
Ohio Historical Society, Columbus
Railroad and Locomotive Historical Society, Waban, Massachusetts
Smithsonian Institution, Washington, D.C.
United States Patent Office, Washington, D.C.

A great number of state, county and local historical societies, highway departments, officials, civic groups and history-minded individuals contributed a wealth of material. Others unstintingly gave of their time and the results of their personal researches, among them:

ILLINOISANS
O. M. Brodfueherer
Miss Thelma Eaton
Frank F. Fowle
Lewis A. Harlow
James F. O'Gorman
S. E. Reed
Miss Jean Sellers

INDIANANS
Eugene R. Bock
Miss Janet Davis
John T. Dizer
Mrs. W. H. Herzler
Alvin W. Holmes
Frederick Polley
Sidney B. Pepe
Robert B. Yule

IOWANS
Don L. Berry
C. V. Simon

JERSEYITES
George W. Armstrong
Mrs. Albert Day
Mrs. Lucy G. Kemp

KANSANS
Ashley B. Taylor
W. A. Stacey

MARYLANDERS
Mr. and Mrs. John W. Poteet
H. Grattan K. Tyrrell

MICHIGANERS
William J. Duchaine
Duane L. Riley
Miss Priscilla Stockwell
Miss Elizabeth Thompson

MINNESOTAN
Robert A. Hagen

NEW ENGLANDERS
Roy Brooks
Mr. and Mrs. Neil M. Clark
Michael De Vito
Mr. and Mrs. Harold F. Eastman
Mrs. Herbert G. Foster
Mrs. Hiram R. Gatchell
Miss Charlotte P. Goddard
Roger D. Griffin
Mrs. Dorothy P. Harvey
Mr. and Mrs. Orrin H. Lincoln
Leo Litwin
George B. Pease
William Schermerhorn
Mrs. Charles Hadley Watkins

NEW YORKERS
Milton L. Bernstein

Lucius M. Boomer
Dann Chamberlin
Albert B. Corey
E. A. Fessenden
Miss Caroline Sprague
Eugene R. Sulecki
John L. Warner
Harley A. Williams
Frederick C. Wunsch

OHIOANS
Del Axe
E. D. Bates
Mrs. G. J. Baker
Miss Hazel Curschmann
John A. Diehl
Henry A. Gibson
Mrs. Hallie Jones
Mrs. Karl K. Knight
George Laycock
Dwight Leggett
Robert A. Lord
Thomas J. Malone
Terry E. Miller
Howard M. MacKenzie
Eldon M. Neff
Seth Schlotterbeck
Clay Van Winkle
Miss Sara Ruth Watson
Joseph H. Wilson
Mrs. Richard A. Wood

PENNSYLVANIANS
John J. Brindley
Lee H. Nelson
Mr. and Mrs. Harold Sitler
Walter W. Pryse
Raymond E. Wilson

WASHINGTONIAN
(D.C.)
Robert M. Vogel

WEST VIRGINIAN
Herbert B. Nields

WISCONSONIANS
Miss Flora N. Davidson
Francis W. De Sautelle
Delbert Kay

Of the above, especial thanks are due Eugene R. Bock of Anderson, Indiana, my one-time associate, mentor and the foremost authority on covered bridges in the Hoosier State. Also to John A. Diehl, perennial chairman and tabulator of Ohio's Covered Timber Bridge Committee, infatigable researcher Terry Miller of Wooster, Ohio, and more-than-generous Clay Van Winkle of Mt. Vernon, Ohio. Deepest appreciation is also extended to Robert M. Vogel of The Smithsonian Institution, and to the late Dr. Albert B. Corey, Historian of the State of New York.   R.S.A.

ILLUSTRATION CREDITS

The author is grateful to the following people for their permission to use the illustrations in this book. The credits are given alphabetically by source. Allen Collection: 2–4, 11, 21–24, 30, 34, 37, 38, 42, 44, 45, 46c–f, 50, 52–56, 58, 60, 63, 65, 66, 70, 71, 74, 76, 77, 84a–d, 91, 95, 97–100, 112–120, 122, 124, 126, 128a–g, 132, 134, 140, 146, 160, 161, 171, 175, 189, 195, 219, 222, 223, 225, 227, 230, 242, 245–247, 260, 262, 266, 273, 279. Lucy E. Allen: 129, 201. E. W. Bates: 78. Eugene R. Rock: 48, 80, 111, 150, 152, 162, 163, 169, 172, 173, 176, 180, 188, 193, 194, 196, 202, 203, 209, 211–213, 220. John J. Brindley: 32, 57, 59, 61, 62, 64, 69, 73, 130. O. M. Brodfueherer: 216, 217. A. A. Burrows Collection: 281. CF&I Steel Corporation: 277. Chaddock Collection: 67, 131, 133. Dann Chamberlain: 153. Clippinger Studios: 145. M. L. Davies: 1, 143, 149, 151, 154, 157–159, 179, 181, 187, 198, 199, 204, 208, 210, 214, 215, 218. John Diehl: 26, 86, 94, 136, 137, 190. H. F. Eastman Collection: 19. Farmer's Security State Bank: 264. E. A. Fessenden Collection: 110. The Henry Ford Museum: 226. Fowle Collection: 267–272, 274, 275. Free Studio: 276, 278. Henry A. Gibson: 191, 192. William H. Hartley: 35. Mrs. W. H. Herzler: 164, 186. Lena Hiatt Collection: 139. Harry C. Hill: 228. S. Durward Hoag: 83. Alvin W. Holmes: 51, 104–106, 138, 155, 156, 165, 170, 177, 178, 182–185, 197, 200, 207. Edward Hungerford: 68. Delbert Kay: 167, 259. Mrs. K. K. Knight Collection: 18. Lansing Michigan State Journal: 221. Dwight Leggett: 33. Robert A. Lord Collection: 17. Thomas J. Malone Collection: 25. National Cash Register Company: 101–103. Eldon M. Neff: 9, 12, 13, 15, 36, 39, 41, 43, 46a–b, 49, 88–90, 93, 96, 107–109, 127, 205, 206. H. B. Nields Collection: 5, 6, 11a, 16, 79, 81, 82, 92, 121, 123, 125, 135, 141, 142, 144, 174, 231, 258. Ohio Department of Public Works: 31. Orange Nichols: 87. Sidney Pepe: 147, 148, 233–236, 239–241, 284. Frederick Polley: 166. Seth Schlotterbeck: 28, 29, 47. Alvin R. Schwab Collection: 238, 243. Scientific American: 7. Jean Sellers: 244. C. V. Simon: 282, 283. Smithsonian Institution: 14, 232, 265, 280. Caroline Sprague Collection: 27. W. A. Stacey: 263. Priscilla T. Stockwell: 229. William Taylor: 224. Thomas Collection: 8, 10, 168, 237. Warren Ohio Tribune-Chronicle: Frontis. Joe E. Wilson Collection: 40, 72, 75. Wisconsin Conservation Department: 261. Works Progress Administration: 85.

CONTENTS

On Dusty Creaking Planks

MAN, Mother Nature and Father Time have claimed heavy toll on the depleted ranks of covered bridges. In some areas determined effort has managed to continue their existence. In others only the vagaries of geography and the changing paths of travel have combined to aid in their retention.

Since few urban covered bridges survive in the Middle West, the old roofed structures have gradually become a symbol of pastoral countryside. "What a romantic old place!" exclaims the casual tourist who happens upon a timbered tunnel in the course of a back-road ramble.

It is cool within. Robins build nests where the rafters intersect, pausing only to chase away a marauding squirrel whose hideaway is behind a patchwork of shingles. Dauber wasps construct mud hovels along a beam, while from an eave hangs an enormous abode of yellow jackets. On other timbers country swains have carved initials with hearts and arrows. Faded posters proclaim the delights of long-ago fairs and exhibitions, and extol the powers of forgotten nostrums.

How did these bridges come to be, all scattered across the American heartland? It is part of the story of restless pioneers, pressing westward to shape the destiny of a nation.

The first decades of the nineteenth century brought a great era of migration and expansion for young America. Virtually every householder in the East turned his eyes to the new West, and at least thought of going there. A great many pulled up stakes and braved the journey.

This was the same period during which covered wooden bridges were first built and developed. Enterprising artisans in wood carried the knowledge of covered-bridge building over the Appalachian mountain barrier into the newly organized states of the Midwest.

Carpenters from New England, engineer trainees from Pennsylvania and building contractors from New York State all poured into the new territories. There they proceeded to make the landscape as near as possible a duplication of the older regions they had left behind. The abundance of good timber and the many streams to be crossed made it all possible. With the Eastern Seaboard furnishing men, energy and know-how, it was in the Middle West that covered-bridge building in America reached a peak of production and perfection.

For many whose roots are in these states, the memory of covered bridges is stronger than the reality of their continued existence.

"Make a wish and hold your breath as we go through. If you can hold it all the way your wish will come true!" With a short bridge this was all fine, but the larger ones led to popping eyes and scarlet faces.

The covered bridges were scary places at night.

"Screw up your courage. Whistle a merry tune. Or better yet, run through lickety-split!" A retired Ohioan looks rueful. "I tried that," he remembers. "It was a wet night and the bridge was black as a miser's heart. I ran. All of a sudden there was a terrible squawk, and I stumbled over an old hen that'd wandered in out of the rain. I was picking splinters out of my arms, and manure out of my hair for days. And I skinned both knees out of my Sunday pants!"

"Kiss your girl when you go through. A short peck'll do for a short bridge, but if it's long and dark there's time enough for a hug n'squeeze." The elderly Hoosier says nothing, but his thoughts go back to Sunday afternoon buggy rides in 1910, and he smiles.

Covered bridges have been the locale of weddings, church suppers, band concerts and memorable bare-knuckle fist fights. On the darker side the bridges have figured in murders, suicides and lynching parties.

Only memories for most people, yet over three hundred covered bridges are still standing in the states comprising the Middle West.

Due to the work of state highway departments, historical commissions and the half-dozen societies devoted to their recording and preservation, the remaining spans can now easily be located and readily reached in most areas. Intertwined with the physical presence of existing structures is a wealth of state, local and engineering history concerned with former covered bridges which once stood nearby.

A leisurely state-by-state examination is perhaps the best way to tell the story of mid-America's covered bridges, proceeding westward, as did the first men who brought roads and bridges to the land.

1. *Interior of Jackson Bridge showing immense arches of 207 feet clear span.*

II

OHIO

For Long the Most

Oнio's 84,000 miles of roads have hundreds of stream crossings which once did, or still do, provide attractive settings for covered bridges. With varied topography, the state is full of surprising bridge sites.

In the north, the streams run in deep-cut valleys approached by the descent of long steep hills. Occasionally, there is a bridge which spans an unexpected, spectacular ravine.

To the south, in the valley of the river which gives its name to Ohio, the scenes are reminiscent of adjacent Pennsylvania and West Virginia: winding rivers with wooded banks, complete with a covered bridge appearing around a bend as an almost predictable part of the landscape.

More startling are the bridges of the central and northwestern counties of Buckeyeland. Here the roads go straight for miles, imperceptibly climbing and descending. The streams seem to appear from nowhere, winding across the country and changing level only a few feet to the mile. Intersecting highway and river, something barn-like looms up on the horizon, visible for miles, stark on the flat land. Only close approach distinguishes the structure as a covered bridge.

It is doubtful that any other highway crossing built in Ohio can even remotely compare with the economical transportation furnished by

2. *Little covered bridge once served as a gateway in entering Lima, Ohio.*

Lima.

3. Old double-barrel bridge across the Miami River between Hamilton and Rossville, Ohio.

covered bridges. A conservative guess is that the state once had well over 2000. Compiled in 1937, the first published listing gave a total of 609, with nearly a hundred on the 12,000-mile state highway system. Due to deficiencies in the count, the actual number at the time was probably closer to 700. Even as late as 1951, a privately taken census of Ohio covered bridges came to 399.

Generally ignored and unpublicized was the fact that until recent years it was Ohio, not Vermont or any of the New England states, which led the nation in total number of covered bridges.

During the 1950's the figure dropped drastically. Nearly all the roofed spans on state highways were eliminated. Flood-control dams and recreation reservoirs necessitated destruction of dozens, and the toll of time, occasional high water, fire and ever-present wanton vandalism brought the list far down.

By the '60's Pennsylvania, original birthplace of the covered bridge in America, had replaced its western neighbor as the country's top state for the greatest number of structures of this type. Though now in second place, with less than 200 remaining, Ohio still has a fine variety of covered bridges to be searched out by visitors, and in addition can point to many sites of historical importance in covered-bridge history.

Ohio's earliest bridges were not intended to have any degree of permanence; they were largely thrown together in haste with the thought of getting the region open to settlement. For the most part they were open-deck structures, supported by natural stone outcroppings and trestle-

work. For the larger rivers, speedily erected continuous spans on cribbed piling and bents sufficed. Occasionally, a builder with a flair would give his roadway a bit of camber by using naturally curved timbers. This probably accounts for "an arch bridge of 150 feet" across the mouth of the Little Muskingum River, which was soon demolished by a freshet in 1808.

The profit to be gained by bridging important streams at judicious places was readily apparent to early Ohioans. Toll-gathering concessions granted by the state legislature could (and did) make some wealthy men. Other promoters were content to simply have a toll bridge as a traffic inducer, along with a local tavern and general store.

In 1809 John Bever and Thomas Moore received legislative sanction to erect a bridge at their grist and saw mill site on Little Beaver Creek in Columbiana County. The act stated that if they "shall build and complete a bridge with handrails on the sides . . . sufficient for the passage of wagons . . . and continue to keep said bridge in repair, then this act shall be in force for the term of fifty years."

It would appear to be reasonably certain that Messrs. Bever and Moore put handrails on their bridge, which was located about a mile up Little Beaver from its confluence with the Ohio River. A contemporary (1814) report describes this bridge as arched, substantially made, and "well covered in." This last allusion leads to controversy. Quite likely the writer was referring to the boarding, or enclosure of the handrails at the sides. If there was anything as novel as a roof on the bridge (only four years after the first covered bridge was erected in the United States), it would seem that this fact would have been recorded explicitly.

4. Sidewalked crossing of Grand River at Painesville, Ohio.

5. 1836 toll bridge over west channel of Ohio River opposite Wheeling, W. Va. First and only covered bridge to span any part of the Ohio River and only interstate covered bridge to link Ohio with West Virginia (then Virginia).

Unless other, more descriptive accounts or a contemporary drawing can be found at this late date, the question can never truly be answered. That many knowledgeable historians believe the Little Beaver Toll Bridge to have been the "first covered bridge erected in Ohio" is attested by the fact that the site has been so marked by a recent state historical marker.

Other early toll bridges in Ohio included the first Putnam (Zanesville) bridge across the Muskingum, erected in 1812, and another uncovered crossing a little upstream at the forks, built in 1813–14 by architect Rufus Scott.

Over on the Scioto River in the center of the new state was Franklinton, a pioneer village established by a surveyor from Virginia named Lucas Sullivant. Together with a local group, Sullivant hatched a scheme for building a new Ohio state capitol on the high banks east of the river. The legislators, dissatisfied with Chillicothe and Zanesville, approved the move just before the War of 1812. Despite the hostilities, Sullivant commenced erecting a toll bridge across the Scioto, and had it ready for the lawmakers' first session in the new two-story brick capitol build-

ing in December, 1816.

The day of the covered bridge in Ohio dawned with the erection of another Scioto River bridge at the old capital of Chillicothe. Again, it was a toll bridge, financed by a citizen group, and its erection was superintended by Eli Fox, a Connecticut Yankee shipbuilder and millwright who

6. Chillicothe, Ohio, covered bridge of 1817.

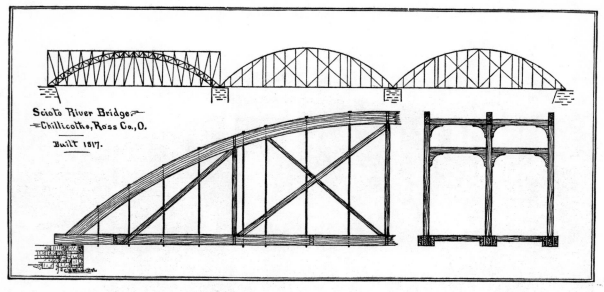

7. Eli Fox's Chillicothe, Ohio, replica of Theodore Burr's Trenton, N.J., masterwork.

had previously worked at bridge-building in Pennsylvania.

Mr. Fox most certainly was familiar with the experimental bridge erected over the Delaware River at Trenton, New Jersey, a 1008-foot, five-span bridge composed of huge laminated arches from which the floor was hung by iron rods.

Built by Theodore Burr in 1805, it was America's second covered bridge.

Adopting the principles of Burr's masterpiece, Mr. Fox fashioned his Chillicothe replica with two spans of 150 feet each. These were composed of three untrussed arches, each with 10 layers of 10 × 2-inch oak, and bottom chords which meas-

8. Plaque at Cambridge commemorates old bridge of 1828–1913 and utilizes masonry and capstone of old horse trough.

9. National Road bridge over Wills Creek at Cambridge, Ohio, stood from 1828 to 1913. This structure utilized the talents of inventor Ithiel Town, designer Lewis Wernwag and architect J. P. Shannon.

11. Sketch by Alexander J. Davis for Columbus, Ohio, Bridge, which was adapted later for use in 1839 bridge truss booklet by Ithiel Town.

10. Old sketch of ornate but advertisement-plastered portal of Cambridge Bridge, with stone watering trough.

ured 10″ × 24″. Authorities agree that the bridge was securely protected with a roof and siding, although these may have been added at a date some time later. The original bridge was completed in November 1817. A third, conventional Burr arch span of similar dimension was added on the north end in 1844. The entire bridge, with uneven roofline, did service for almost seventy years. When Ross County's commissioners decreed its replacement in 1886, the old pioneer spans had to be "dismantled" by purposeful burning.

Another crossing which was the site of a very early Ohio roofed bridge was Dayton's Bridge Street, now called Dayton View or Stratford Avenue. Here in 1818 Nathan S. Hunt of Hamilton, Ohio built a two-span, double-laned covered bridge across the Great Miami River.

Soon a new artery of commerce began inching its way across the state. This was the National Road, one of the Federal Government's earliest and most important civil engineering projects. Built to link the Atlantic seaboard with the newly settled western states, it eventually cost some $7 million and extended from Baltimore almost to the Mississippi River. Along its dusty miles ran the course of empire.

Originally ordered by Congress in 1806, it took nearly fifteen years for the National Road to be finished to the Ohio River. From Wheeling to

Zanesville it followed the pioneer trail called Zane's Trace, but beyond the Muskingum the surveyors projected the route straight west, through infant Columbus and Indianapolis, on to Vandalia, Illinois. To merchants and would-be users, the road's snail-like progress of completion must have seemed interminable. Clearing, grubbing and road-building were all done by men and horses, with primitive stump pullers and grading machinery.

Between Wheeling and Zanesville, the National Road's bridging was for the most part of massive masonry, painstakingly fitted and mortared to last for decades. Unique were the odd "S" bridges, stone-parapeted arch spans built at right angles to a stream where the normally straight highway came obliquely to the crossing. The meticulous masons who built them also provided the substructure for the longer wooden bridges on the road, and in some cases their handiwork still supports the modern bridges of U.S. 40 and Ohio 440 today.

Only one wooden bridge of consequence was built on the first section of the National Road in Ohio—the double-barreled crossing of Wills Creek at Cambridge, erected in 1828. Designs for this structure were furnished by Lewis Wernwag of Harpers Ferry, Virginia, the famed builder of great arch bridges elsewhere. Wernwag's plan for Cambridge was in the nature

11a. (See also 11) Town & Davis' lattice fabrication took Broad Street across the Scioto River at Columbus.

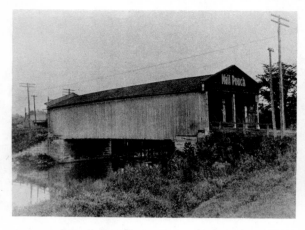

12. National Road bridge over Buck Creek west of Springfield, Ohio.

13. Traffic was light enough in 1905 to use the left lane without fear of collision. National Road bridge over Beaver Creek east of Harmony, Ohio.

of a concession to an innovation in bridge-building technique. The old master-builder specified Connecticut architect Ithiel Town's patent lattice "mode" of bridge truss for this one, the only known place at which he tried this type.

The actual fabrication of the Cambridge span fell to J. P. Shannon, with Wernwag credited as the "architect." The professionals need have had no reservations about using the new-fangled Town lattice truss. The Shannon-Wernwag double-barreled bridge at Cambridge stood until replaced in 1913.

Ithiel Town himself, assisted by his partner Alexander J. Davis, drew the plans for the National Road bridge which would grace the capital city of Columbus. This was to span the Scioto at the foot of Broad Street, where Lucas

Sullivant had foresightedly connected the city with old Franklinton. Sullivant's heirs received some $10,000 for the old river crossing and its franchise.

The new National Road bridge was a real showcase for the talents of the patentee, with a double roadway and arcaded sidewalks along each side. Town and Davis had the portals embellished with "a very rich style of exterior finish," consisting of colonnades and simulated stonework, surmounted by a rounded pediment topped by acroteria. Mr. Town modestly commented that "it is presumed that no other object of the kind in the country would surpass it in grandeur."

This imposing structure, which would have been a credit to even a European capital, stretched 280 feet in two spans across the Scioto.

14. Moscow Bridge east of Hebron, Ohio, carried National Road Traffic for nearly a century.

15. Mad River Bridge near Springfield, Ohio, served National Road until 1932.

Superintending its construction was Captain Henry F. Brewerton, a West Pointer, assisted by two young lieutenants from the Corps of Engineers. Their labors kept them in Columbus for two years (1832–34). Ithiel Town's "rich design" went on to serve the capital and the National Road for nearly half a century.

At least seventeen covered bridges were built on the National Road between Zanesville and the Indiana line, most of them with two lanes in anticipation of heavy traffic. Beyond Springfield were a series of four bridges on the lattice plan. For use in the building of these, a Mrs. Herr of Donnelsville is said to have produced thousands of wooden trunnels. With the assistance of a son she laboriously turned them out on a hand lathe, working a subcontract for the bridge builders.

Ironically, even as it was pushed westward across Ohio between 1828 and 1840, the National Road was being outmoded. New canals and railroads tapped the potential travel which might have moved over it. The road was never actually finished, but for a time it was the main artery of Ohio's migration and commerce. Blue-bodied Conestoga wagons, mule trains and Concord coaches went rumbling over its dust-blown distances, punctuated by slow pacing through the cool shade of its covered bridges.

As traffic waned, the road languished and be-

came more useful as a local thoroughfare. Most of the covered bridges on its length stood well into the twentieth century. Beyond Vandalia (Ohio), the crossing of Big Stillwater River survived the great 1913 flood and was kept intact even after the Miami Conservancy District built the Englewood Dam downstream. In order to keep the bridge in place during flood stage periods, iron rods and steel cables were stretched from the upper chord and anchored in the masonry of pier and abutments. For a number of years this arrangement served to keep the old bridge down as well as up. Water at times stood 30 feet above the old National Road, but the bridge took its periodic dunkings gracefully.

With the rebirth of "The Road" as a through highway for automobiles, the cross-state route got back its traffic in the early 1920's. Tin lizzies and elegant touring cars whined their tires on the brick pavements, churned dust on the straightaways, and clattered the planking of the old bridges. One by one the timbered tunnels vanished, to become part of the memories of the National Road. Moscow Bridge over the South Fork of the Licking River east of Hebron was replaced in 1928, after having stood for almost a hundred years. Among the last to go was Springfield's big Mad River crossing, a two-lane lattice which existed until 1932.

16. *The Famous "Y" Bridge at Zanesville, Ohio, built across both the Muskingum and Licking Rivers from designs by Catharinus Buckingham.*

Over in Zanesville, the National Road and its traffic brought about the building of one of Ohio's (and the nation's) most unusual covered bridges. This was the famous old "Y" Bridge, spanning both the Muskingum and Licking rivers.

In 1812 Zanesville was briefly the state's capital. Ohio's lawmakers, commuting from other towns, naturally wished to be rid of the nuisance of ferrying the confluent rivers. They authorized a local group of men to construct a bridge "from the point opposite Main Street to an island at the mouth of the Licking, hence north and south each way across the mouth of Licking Creek." Though at first glance the wording seems strange, the geography was such that the proposed bridge would be a practical method of spanning both streams.

As noted previously, the first bridge on this site was built in 1813–14 by Rufus Scott. It was a flimsy, uncovered structure on wooden trestling and crib piers filled with loose stone. Part of it was swept away by a freshet within six months, and the whole shebang fell into the river in 1818. A second bridge, supposed to have been built with cambered lower chords and perhaps par-

tially covered, took its place only to be condemned after thirteen years of service.

By 1830, construction of the National Road was complete to Zanesville, and it was obvious that traffic across the Muskingum would soon be on the increase. Ebenezer Buckingham and some associates, who already owned the Putnam (or Lower) Bridge at Zanesville, contrived to buy out the stockholders of the Muskingum & Licking Bridge, thus gaining a monopoly on the town's river crossings. All was not well, however, for the Upper Bridge was condemned and an ice-

17. *"Y" Bridge at Zanesville, Ohio.*

flood the following winter further weakened it.

Buckingham's son Catharinus was a graduate of the United States Military Academy, and had stayed on for a year at the Point to teach natural philosophy. Upon the young man's return to Zanesville, the father engaged him in drawing up plans for a new bridge at the upper crossing.

Catharinus made a small wooden model to scale, 7 feet long, with its biggest timber 1 × ½-inch. Under Ebenezer's parental eye, the West Pointer exhibited this to the assembled bridge company directors. First he tested it by placing weight amounting to 500 pounds upon it. When the onlookers still appeared skeptical, Buckingham and an assistant stood on the model and deliberately "surged" on it with their whole weight. Nothing broke.

This is one of the earliest records of a feat of this kind, which was also carried out with success by later bridge builders in New Hampshire, West Virginia and Indiana. Catharinus Buckingham of Ohio managed to achieve considerable local fame by this unorthodox method of showing off his first (and only) bridge.

The Buckinghams immediately set about to build their new bridge, a job which entailed all new masonry as well as superstructure. During the summer of 1832 Catharinus Buckingham was struck down with cholera and lay near death for days. Ebenezer took over superintendence at the bridge site, tending to his sick son at night.

On the morning of August 21, one of the new spans of the bridge was noted to have moved over about six inches. Ebenezer anxiously conferred with Catharinus at noon; what he didn't know was that the span was resting on the "wretched masonry" of one of the old piers. In midafternoon the span fell without warning. Four men ran off as the framework toppled and wrenched loose. Seven clung to the floating wreckage and were rescued when it grounded beyond the Lower Bridge. Ebenezer Buckingham and a workman named Jacob Boyd were either killed by falling timbers or drowned.

Despite the shock of his father's death, young Catharinus Buckingham recovered from his illness and completed the bridge by December. It was founded on a huge center pier with circular

18. Lesser-known Putnam or Lower Bridge at Zanesville, Ohio, flanked by covered wooden railroad bridge.

19. *Massive circular pier under toll house in middle of Zanesville's "Y" Bridge. It gave up treasure of lost coins on demolition in 1901.*

walls eight feet thick. From this base the bridge stretched three spans across the Muskingum to the east (or Zanesville) shore, and a like number to the north bank of the Licking. The main route extended on another two spans to complete the crossing of the converging rivers. Surprisingly, the bridge trusses were framed with heavy multiple kingposts, but did not make use of arches.

Travelers westward on the National Road received rather strange directions: "Go to the middle of the bridge and turn left!" Since the toll booth was also in the center of the bridge, they had to stop anyway.

From the beginning the Buckinghams and other stockholders received handsome dividends from their two toll bridges at Zanesville, and not until 1868 were the bridges freed to the tune of a $43,800 settlement.

Dozens of old coins were later found in the hollow center pier, where they had slipped through the floorboards from the fingers of generations of toll-payers and toll-takers. Descendants of the stockholders laid no claim to the lost loot, and the money went as souvenirs to the workmen engaged in demolishing the old bridge in 1901.

Zanesville's old landmark was a remarkably tough bridge. During its last quarter-century it even supported a trolley-car line. Strangely, for most of its existence, this "bifurcated bridge" was known as either the "Muskingum & Licking" or simply the "Upper" bridge. Calling it "Y", as its concrete successor is known today, began only in its declining years. Though covered bridges at

Harpers Ferry, Virginia, Lyons Falls, New York, and Phillipsburg, New Jersey had similar three-pronged features, there has never been another structure quite like Zanesville's old "Y".

Catharinus Buckingham, despite his auspicious entry into bridge design, apparently never built another bridge. He taught mathematics for a spell at Kenyon College and then became a successful Chicago businessman. At various places in Ohio, references to a type of bridge termed a "Buckingham" crop up in old proposals. Both Ebenezer and Catharinus were well-known Ohioans, and their bridge at Zanesville was a notable landmark for seventy years. It may well be that local builders, familiar with the famed structure, adopted the features of its tough-timbered multiple-kingpost trusses, and termed this method of boxed framing without the use of arches a "Buckingham" truss.

Up in the Western Reserve country of northern Ohio, population growth was slow. Transportation was mainly by boat along the shore of Lake Erie, and communication with the rest of Ohio was very sporadic. Cleaveland (the "a" was dropped in 1832) had less than 1000 people in 1830, and its southern water artery to link the Great Lakes with the Ohio River was still incomplete. When the Ohio & Erie Canal was finally finished it brought new towns, new prosperity and city rivalry.

Across the Cuyahoga River from what is now downtown Cleveland was a thriving settlement called Ohio City. Cleveland's western gateway

20. *Cleveland's covered bridge across the Cuyahoga River, scene of dissension and battle in 1835.*

21. Two-lane bridge was prominent landmark of Milford, Ohio, in the 1850's.

was a floating bridge at Detroit Street (Avenue), directly connecting the towns. By 1835 land promoter James S. Clark and some associates had acquired a sizable allotment south of Ohio City. Clark extended Columbia Street to the Cuyahoga, and Cleveland's authorities responded by laying Columbus Road down the narrow neck of land on their side of the river. The next step was to erect a bridge. This Clark proceeded to do in 1834–35.

The new crossing was a covered bridge with two 100-foot spans divided by an open center draw sufficient for the passage of a vessel with 49-foot beam. The bridges were a commodious 33 feet in width. In order to complete the streets and causeway leading to the bridge, Clark's men utilized a sizable gravel bank, laid a railway, and drew earth through the bridge on small dump cars. Thus Cleveland's first covered bridge had the further distinction of being the first in Ohio and one of the first in the nation to be laid with

railroad track. Though chartered as a toll bridge, upon completion the owners presented the new structure to Cleveland with the stipulation that it should remain forever free.

22. Montgomery Pike out of Cincinnati once bridged Little Miami River at Foster's Crossing, Ohio.

Residents of Ohio City resented the new bridge, since westward travel now bypassed their town. To add to their ire, half of their old floating bridge was quietly removed by persons unknown one night in the dark of the moon. Small portions of it were later discovered bobbing in Lake Erie.

Ohio Citians took up the cry of "Two Bridges or None!" and their city council adopted a resolution to the effect that the new bridge to the south was a public nuisance. Following up the motion came drastic action. On October 27, 1837 Ohio City's marshal and some hot-headed deputies set off a blast of black powder under the west end of the bridge. To their disappointment the damage was slight. Next, they cut a huge ditch across the causeway, effectively blocking use of the crossing. Finally, to top it off, a thousand men, some armed, assembled to tear the hateful bridge asunder.

Meanwhile, Clevelanders had not been idle. They gathered on their own side of the Cuyahoga, evidencing displeasure at the state of affairs by drawing up an old cannon, usually put to use only for celebration of the Glorious Fourth. Backing the field piece was a company

23. Double-barrel bridge with massive masonry approaches stood over Paint Creek east of Bainbridge, Ohio.

of militia, some with loaded muskets.

With a big wooden screen for protection, the Ohio City boys went to work on the offending bridge with ringing axes and clanging crowbars. The Cleveland militia charged. In the melee of fisticuffs and bloodied noses, somebody spiked the cannon with an old file.

Fortunately the county sheriff soon put in an appearance and read the riot act to the warring citizens. No casualties were reported, but it was a near thing. Under constant guard, the bridge was repaired and kept in use under a court

24. Town lattice turnpike bridge over Rock Creek in Ashtabula County, Ohio, served for 116 years.

25. *Early photo shows Sandusky River Bridge on State Street in Fremont, Ohio.*

Other more isolated double-barrels were a feature of the landscape east of Bainbridge, spanning Paint Creek, over the North Fork of the same stream west of New Holland, and the crossing of Mad River west of Urbana in Champaign County.

In Ashtabula County's village of Rock Creek one old two-lane Town lattice span stood until 1948. This was a real pioneer, having been built in 1832 for the Ashtabula and Trumbull Turnpike Company by Samuel Ackley and George Crowell.

Growing settlements thought the divided lane a good feature to incorporate into local covered bridges. Among these were Fremont, Monroeville, Milan, Kent and Newton Falls in the northern part of the state, and Hamilton and Dayton

decree. The intercity grudge refused to fade, and died hard even when Ohio City was finally annexed to Cleveland in 1854. The cause of all the furore, Cleveland's only covered bridge of record, was extensively rebuilt in 1846, and gave way to an iron drawbridge in 1870.

The commodious double-barreled bridges of the National Road have already been mentioned. Other turnpikes also used them, particularly the toll roads which were built spoke-fashion out of Cincinnati. There was one at Milford, and another on the Montgomery Pike at Foster's Crossing, both spanning the Little Miami River. To the west were even larger two-lane bridges, over the Great Miami and Dry Fork on the Harrison Pike.

26. *Wiley and Glover's "Red Bridge" at Fairhaven, Ohio, was victim of runaway potato truck.*

27. *Twin-tunneled span over Huron River at Monroeville, Ohio, was originally erected in 1836.*

in southern Ohio. To the west of Dayton, Preble County once had five double-lane covered bridges within its borders. That at Fairhaven over Four Mile Creek once sported a cryptic sign proclaiming:

> The genius of Man
> Is Hard to Discover.
> This bridge was Built
> By Wiley and Glover.

For years the Wiley-Glover double-barrel was kept well painted in red. During a repair job the scheme was changed to white, but local people persisted in referring to the Fairhaven structure as "Red Bridge" for the balance of its days. At

28. *Near site is grave of Orlistus Roberts, builder of Roberts Bridge.*

the age of ninety-three, a runaway truckload of potatoes sent it crashing into the creek it had spanned so long.

Also in Preble County, and a prime attraction today, is the state's sole surviving example of the two-lane covered bridge. Three miles south of Eaton is the Roberts Bridge, spanning Seven Mile Creek on the old Camden Pike. It was erected in 1829–30 by Orlistus Roberts, a Yankee carpenter, cabinet and clockmaker from Bristol, Connecticut. Roberts had a farm and shop near the bridge site, and tried his hand at heavy con-

struction when he took the contract for its erection. Unhappily, before the 3-span Burr arch truss was finished, Roberts took sick and died. The bridge was completed by his seventeen-year-old apprentice, Joseph Libran Campbell, who also married his widow.

Now well launched into its second century, the 91-foot Roberts Bridge has been restored by the Preble County Commissioners. They were spurred on by local interest spearheaded by former County Maintenance Engineer Seth S. Schlotterbeck, who in turn was aided and abetted by both the Northern and Southern Ohio Covered Bridge Associations. It is a shining (literally, with bright red paint) example of what can be accomplished in the way of saving an outstanding bridge and irreplaceable landmark.

Probably considered as "just another country bridge" when it was built, the Roberts Bridge is one of only six double-barreled covered bridges existing in the United States today. It also ranks among the oldest covered bridges of authenticated date in the nation, one of four erected before 1830. It may well someday be the oldest. Certainly, it is now America's oldest covered bridge outside of New England.

It was its extensive network of canals which bound Ohio together and forged it into a unified state. There were two main routes, the 248-mile Miami & Erie between Toledo and Cincinnati, and the Ohio & Erie, which extended 308 miles from Cleveland to Portsmouth. Hundreds and hundreds of boats clustered and clogged the canals in their heyday, and the waterways were the making of such towns as Akron, Newark and Hamilton.

29. *Roberts Bridge over Seven Mile Creek on Camden Pike south of Eaton, Ohio, is one of six double-barrel covered bridges in the United States today, and also one of the oldest (1829–30) in the nation. This old view shows appearance in 1895.*

30. *Roberts Bridge in 1946 prior to restoration.*

31. Covered wooden aqueduct of Miami & Erie Canal at Taylorsville, Ohio. Burr arch trusswork is revealed at time of collapse.

Financing canals was a continuous drain on state monies. In New York and Pennsylvania locks and aqueducts were built on a grand and permanent style, completely of stone. Not only to cut costs, but to speed completion, the Ohio canal builders depended on wooden structures. Though they soon rotted and needed early replacement, wooden locks sufficed, along with deep wooden troughs for open aqueducts, set on crib piers.

Occasionally the canals resorted to more elaborate superstructures, such as covered wooden aqueducts. On the Ohio & Erie, the main crossing of the Scioto River was one of these, located just south of Circleville. Gliding through the long dim watery tunnel high above the river was an adventure for packet-boat passengers. When the waterway was closed to navigation in the winter, the frozen trunk of the aqueduct offered a sheltered place for skating.

Over on the Miami Canal was another sizable covered aqueduct. Three spans of Burr truss supported a deep but always leaky trunk, with a towpath on the side. This structure stood at Taylorsville, near Vandalia, and spanned the Great Miami River.

Also necessary were covered highway bridges over the canals, and a great number of these served not only local highways but individual farms along the routes of the waterways. On private and lightly traveled crossings there were sometimes hinged trap doors installed in the bridge floors. Protected from the weather, loads of grain and potatoes could be dumped directly from farm wagons into the hold of a canal boat positioned below.

With abandonment of the Ohio canals at the beginning of the present century, the aqueducts rotted and collapsed, or were deliberately burned. Most of the highway bridges were razed, but some, particularly in thrifty Fairfield County, were salvaged and re-erected at new sites.

Today only one covered bridge still spans the old dry bed of the Ohio & Erie Canal. It is a private structure, probably erected during the leisurely latter days of canal operation. Shorn of most of its siding, it is located on the Barger Farm near Omega in Pike County.

Much of Ohio's covered-bridge history is concerned with the people who built and were responsible for their existence. Theodore Burr never set foot in the state, but his patent arched-truss bridges were copied and built here in a variety of modifications.

In at least twelve counties of Ohio, Ithiel Town's lattice bridges enjoyed a spotty popularity. With the showy Scioto River crossing at Columbus, and half a dozen more at other loca-

32. *Doyle or Mullen Road Bridge near Jefferson, Ohio, one of Ashtabula County's fifteen remaining spans.*

tions on the National Road, Town had good examples in the field. Selling the plan to local builders was carried out by agents employed on a commission basis by the patentee, operating from offices in Washington, New York and his home town, New Haven, Connecticut.

Due to the widespread use of the Town mode in New England, it was only natural that Yankee settlers in northern Ohio should elect to use the familiar type. Along the Lake Erie shore, with deep-channeled streams feeding northward, the Town bridge found its greatest popularity. In Ashtabula County wooden-pinned lattices were still being erected long after Town died. In central Ohio, the Town type was among the very last of the "old" (nonreplica) covered bridges to be built. The firm of Creager and Kober used

a neat bolted lattice adaption which incorporated auxiliary arches and a nearly flat roof. This partnership erected at least two bridges of this design, one near Creola in Vinton County in 1918, and another near Bremen in Fairfield County, which was finished on September 17, 1920.

Colonel Stephen H. Long also managed to get a number of his patented truss bridges erected in Ohio. The Colonel, always busy with regular army duties, set up a system of "sub-agents" directed by his brother Moses of Rochester, New York. Some were bona fide bridge builders and carpenters, but more often they were simply men of importance in their communities who could be counted on to handle business details and to see that Colonel Long received his just royalties.

In 1836, Long listed six such agents in the state of Ohio. There is no record today of Colonel Sherman Peck of Portage County, or Andrew E. and William J. Trumbull of Lower Sandusky (Fremont). "Sabried Dodge, Esq." was apparently a civil engineer with a roving commission to cover all of Buckeyeland. Another of Long's choices was Boaz M. Atherton, an attorney in New Philadelphia. Of Atherton an old history states: "He was well versed in law . . . but lacked what is denominated as a legal mind."

Colonel Long fared better in Marietta, where his sub-agent was Stephen Daniels. Daniels was a house carpenter by trade, born in western New York State. With numerous streams winding

33. *Plans for a typical Ashtabula County, Ohio, town lattice covered bridge.*

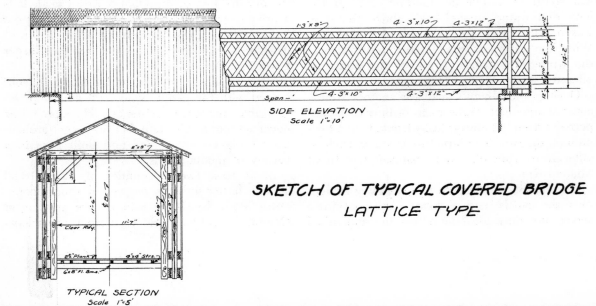

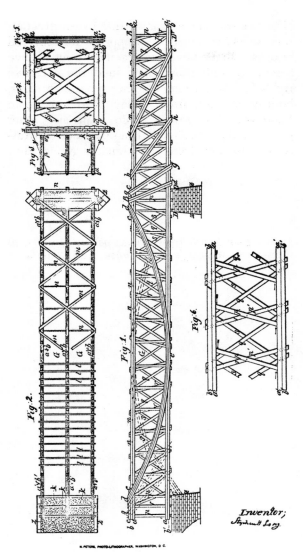

34. *Patent drawing of Col. S. H. Long's wooden suspension arch bridge of 1858. Some were actually built in southern Ohio.*

from continual reference. In time he even got to know the Colonel personally while the latter was stationed in Louisville.

During the 1850's, the Daniels boys went into business for themselves. The older Stephen remained in Marietta, William worked out of Ironton, and young Stephen located in Cincinnati. Joseph, whose grasp of the work of design and framing was apparently the best of the clan, lived for a number of years in Spring Valley, Ohio, and is recorded as the builder of at least six big bridges in Greene and Warren Counties, all on Long's plan. By 1853 he had moved on to Indiana, where his subsequent bridges gained him even greater fame.

While resident in Louisville, Colonel Long was busy supervising the erection of marine hospitals along the Ohio and Mississippi rivers. Somehow he found time to devise still another wooden bridge truss, a sort of culmination of his previous efforts. Patented in 1858, it was a unique thing, composed of an inverted arch acting in suspension, tied to Long's regular framed truss of proven worth. The bridge could also be augmented by the addition of a regular bowstring arch as well.

At least two of these strange all-wooden suspension bridges were built, and stood over Raccoon Creek in Gallia County, Ohio until recent

35. *Long trusses support the E. L. Dean Bridge over Great Miami River north of Troy, the second longest covered bridge in Ohio today.*

among the wooded hills of southern Ohio, there was a crying need for adequate bridges. Daniels soon switched his profession and became a bridge builder of both ability and renown.

With his three sons, Stephen, Joseph and William, the Marietta man engaged in erecting bridges all over the southern counties of Ohio. His copy of Colonel Long's little booklet of directions to bridge builders became dog-eared

36. *Robert W. Smith, Ohio bridge truss inventor.*

of bridge was so well known that its construction was specified in local proposals for covered bridges. Home-town contractors built Howe trusses, as did firms which held the exclusive rights for the erection of other types of bridges, both wood and iron. Today there are more Howe-truss bridges in Ohio than any other patented type. Scattered from Marietta to Russells Point, and from Ashtabula to Xenia, they

37. *Original Smith truss bridge patent of 1867, as shown on company's Tippecanoe City letterhead.*

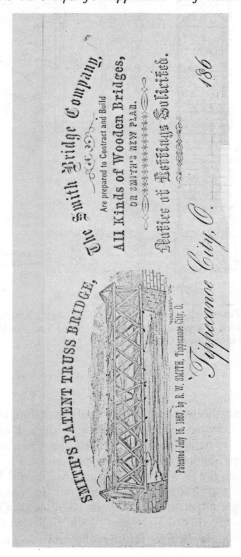

years. One was at Garners Ford, while another which followed the patent drawing almost to the letter was on Ohio Route 775 ten miles southwest of Gallipolis.

Connecting the Daniels family with these bridges is a small model of one section of the "Long Suspension Bridge" of 1858, which was given, along with other family bridge-building mementos, to the Indiana Historical Society in Indianapolis. The name "Stephen Daniels, Marietta, Ohio" is on the model. Since the older Stephen died in 1853, this last venture of Colonel Long into the bridge-patenting business may have been carried out experimentally in Ohio by the younger Daniels, sometime just prior to the Civil War.

Long trusses, based on the Colonel's earlier and more conventional patent, still stand in at least six Ohio counties. Most prominent is the well-preserved E. L. Dean Bridge over the Great Miami River north of Troy, the second longest covered bridge in the state.

Like Theodore Burr, William Howe never visited Ohio, but through relatives his influence on the state's bridges was extensive (see Chapter X). Primarily for the use of the iron horse, his wood-and-iron Howe truss of 1840 was a common crossing on practically every railroad in Ohio. When the patents expired in the 1860's this type

38. *Miami River Bridge at Robert Smith's home town, Tippecanoe City (now Tipp City), Ohio, stood from 1865 to 1915.*

still demonstrate the principles of simplicity and ease of erection which for a time made "the Howe" the most popular type of bridge in the world.

Covered-bridge truss invention and promotion in Ohio was not confined to out-of-staters. There were natives who tirelessly experimented with all available types and evolved some new and better forms of framing.

Foremost of these was Robert W. Smith (1833–98), whose Smith Bridge Company of Toledo vied for building contracts over most of the Middle West. Robert Smith was born in the hamlet of West Charleston in Miami County, son of a cabinet maker from Maryland. Due to the unsettled nature of the times, the boy was educated at home by his mother. At fifteen, he did manage to get inside a schoolhouse to take an intensive six-week course in geometry. This stood him well during a year as a carpenter's apprentice, during which he designed an unusual three-floor continuous stairway. At seventeen, the young man was in business for himself as a house carpenter and barn builder.

Homes for man and beast led Smith to a study of the best forms for heavy construction, and eventually into bridge design. In 1867 the sharp-eyed, bearded builder devised a new type of wooden bridge truss, using a double set of trussed timbers without any tension members. At a time when the wood-and-iron Howe truss was extremely popular, Smith's bridge received a patent and temporarily reversed the trend to iron by successfully eliminating the rods and angle blocks which featured Howe's plan.

Robert Smith founded a company to erect his patent bridges, which originally operated out of Tippecanoe City (now Tipp City), Ohio. Success came immediately, and unlike many inventors, the patentee found ready acceptance on home ground. During 1867–70 his budding firm built over fifteen Smith Patent Bridges right in Miami County. These were in fact all the bridges erected in the county during that time, and the commissioners reported that they "desired nothing better."

Unlike some of his predecessors, Robert Smith realized that his bridge needed a good technical

39. Letterhead of Smith Bridge Company after removal to Toledo, Ohio.

knowledge and a bit of special skill to erect. Though he welcomed any patent royalties that came his way, he spent little effort in hawking rights to his invention in distant states. His own company, or trusted associates with offshoot establishments, built the majority of the Smith bridges. Adaptable to railway use and as a smaller half-truss for short farm bridges, the wooden patent types saw service in two dozen Ohio counties of record, as well as in the neighboring states of Pennsylvania, West Virginia and Indiana. During the 1870 decade they went up in profusion, with Smith's representatives putting in low bids at letting after letting.

40. 440-foot Smith type bridge at Conesville, near Coshocton, Ohio, was for years the state's longest.

Notable were a number of big Smith bridges over the Scioto River north of Columbus, and at Nelsonville over the Hocking River. Over the Muskingum the Smith Bridge Company erected the long structure at Lowell, Randles Bridge south of Coshocton, and the well-remembered 440-foot crossing at Conesville. Built at a cost of $7110.45 in 1877, this last was Ohio's longest covered bridge for many years. Condemned for use, particularly by school buses, it was purposely razed by burning in August 1958.

Robert Smith moved his headquarters to Toledo in 1869, and by that year his company had successfully erected over a hundred of the patent bridges. More improvements were added and protected by a new patent, and soon "a Smith" could be erected all in wood, in the newly accepted iron which the inventor had at first scorned, or with a combination of both.

Using good business sense, Smith and his company were not insistent that their own patent trusses be used. If a county, municipality or railroad board wanted a Howe, Post or Whipple type bridge for their site, Smith raised no objections, and would put up a good bridge on any plan. His stock company, organized in 1870, included associates who were excellent bridge builders in their own right. Among them was Albert S. Miller, who later established himself as a builder of Smith-patent trusses in Oregon,

41. *Stevenson Road Bridge north of Xenia, Ohio, use:
a form of the Smith truss.*

42. *1869 Smith patent truss was the most popular of
Robert Smith's designs.*

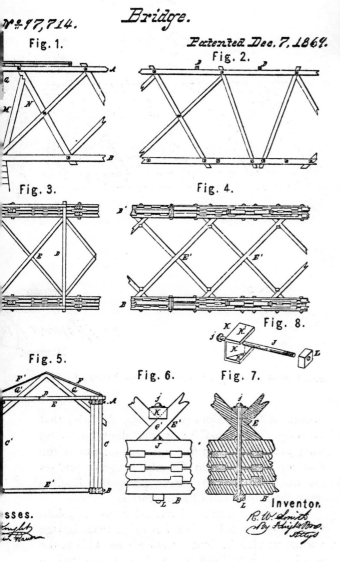

and William H. Gorrill, who laid the groundwork
for the successful Pacific Bridge Company, builders of Smith bridges in California.

The parent firm in Toledo usually assembled
the components of a bridge at their home yard,
shipping them by rail to the prepared site. If
the distance was too great, arrangements were
made to procure and prepare local timber, using
master plans from the home office. Standard
charges for complete covered bridges put up
by Smith's company were:

100 feet	$16.00 per foot
125 feet	$18.00 per foot
150 feet	$20.00 per foot
200 feet	$24.00 per foot

These are of course rough estimates, and when
competition at a bridge letting was strong, the
bids could be lumped considerably lower.
Whether erected by his own men, or occasionally
by others with the know-how and payment of
$1.00 to $1.50 per foot royalty, Robert Smith
guaranteed the efficiency and stability of his
patent design. Nearly thirty of the covered all-
wooden ones are still standing today.

Smith was also active in the invention of draw-
bridges, swinging spans for canals, and floating
ferry docks. By the time the gifted inventor sold
out his construction interests in 1890, the wooden
bridge which had started it all was an obsolete
relic of the past.

43. *Reuben L. Partridge, another Ohio inventor of wooden bridge trusses.*

Generally similar to Smith's patent was one issued to Reuben L. Partridge (1823–1900) of Marysville, Ohio. This 1872 design varied from Smith's in details of timber amounts and angles, and included a special method of securing joints by means of a "bifurcated shoe."

Partridge, born in Wilmington, New York, came to the Ohio country with his widowed mother in 1836. Originally a wagonmaker's apprentice, he gravitated into house carpentry, contracting and bridge-building. One account states that he erected "the first self-supporting

44. *Columbus Bridge Company built Franklin County, Ohio's, sole surviving covered bridge, using Partridge design.*

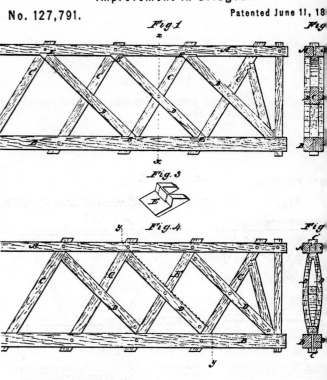

R. L. PARTRIDGE.
Improvement in Bridges.

No. 127,791.   Patented June 11, 18

Fig.1

Fig.3

Fig.4

Witnesses: Inventor:

45. *Patent drawing of the Partridge Truss of 1872.*

bridge in Union County" in 1855. A claim that Partridge built "200" bridges is doubtless a bit exaggerated. Though the dates are unknown, the five remaining Union County covered bridges are on the Partridge patent plan, and Reuben more than likely built them himself.

Over near Canal Winchester in Franklin County is the only other Partridge truss bridge known to exist in Ohio or elsewhere. This is the sturdy 134-foot Bergstresser Bridge, erected in 1887 by a local firm called the Columbus Bridge Company.

46a. *Big Darby Creek Bridge, now by-passed.*

46b. *Old bridge over Big Darby Creek.*

46c. *Big Darby Creek Bridge.*

46d. *Spain Creek road bridge.*

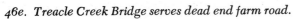

46e. *Treacle Creek Bridge serves dead end farm road.*

46f. *Little Darby Creek Bridge south of Milford Center.*

Mustached, kindly Reuben Partridge is one of the few recorded bridge builders who actually gave his life to his profession. One day in 1900 he fell through the timbers of a bridge over Blues Creek and was fatally injured.

Though an innovator himself, Evrett S. Sherman of Galena and later Eaton, Ohio, was a builder who seems to have preferred the designs of others. He patented a small simple highway truss of his own, but his better-known, more substantial covered bridges followed the little-known Childs patent.

A native of Henniker, New Hampshire, Horace Childs is principally noted as a builder of bridges on the plans of Colonel Stephen H. Long, to whom he was related by marriage. Childs' own wooden-bridge patent of 1846 employed the use of iron rods as counterbraces, a wrinkle in trusses previously untried by designers. Though the inventor was a prominent New England railroad bridge contractor, no record so far has turned up of any of the Childs-patent truss types ever being built in the Northeast. The only known examples, past or present, were erected in Ohio. This is partially accounted for by Evrett Sherman, like Childs a New Hampshireman, who was probably familiar with the obscure patent obtained by the railroad contractor.

After the Civil War, Mr. Sherman appeared in Ohio, contracting for bridges in Madison and later Delaware County. By the 1880's he was in Preble County, where he was responsible for at least twenty of the unusual Childs-type

47. Evrett S. Sherman, New Hampshireman who brought the Childs patent truss to Ohio.

bridges. Erected long after the patent had expired, and containing some variations doubtless devised by Mr. Sherman, there are seven of these bridges standing today in Preble County, all erected between 1887 and 1895. Another, earlier example is located north of Olive Green in Delaware County.

Among specialists in the trade were men like stern-visaged, neck-whiskered Jacob Morgan of

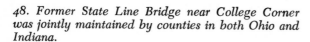

48. Former State Line Bridge near College Corner was jointly maintained by counties in both Ohio and Indiana.

49. Interior of State Line Bridge, showing Childs truss.

50. *Unusually lengthy former bridge over Twin Creek near Gratis, Ohio.*

51. *Adaption of Childs truss in E. S. Sherman's Twin Creek Bridge near Gratis, Ohio (1868–1947).*

Dundee, who bridged the streams of Tuscarawas County during the 1850's and '60's. The majority of his bridges were recorded in old records as on the "Buckingham" plan of heavy multiple kingpost framing. He was succeeded in this work by Jordan Hall Banks (1843–1917) of New Cumberland, a Civil War veteran who had survived the horrors of both Libby and Andersonville prisons. Banks-built bridges of the 1870 period also followed the well-established Buckingham truss arrangement. For thirty years Jordan Banks was Tuscarawas County's principal covered-bridge contractor and repairer. An active man in his chosen work, he built solidly and well. Even the scaffoldings for his bridges had to be of exceptional strength, for it is recorded that Banks tipped the scales at some 375 pounds!

Also typical of Ohio's local builders were Jacob R. Brandt and James W. Buchanan, whose work centered in Fairfield County. Brandt (1836–1911) lived on a farm west of Lancaster, where he utilized a long lane for laying out bridge timbers. When a pair of trusses were satisfactory in his judgment, Brandt would hire teamsters to haul the prefabricated pieces to a bridge site, there to be assembled, roofed and sided.

Known as "Cap" because of his Civil War service, Jacob Brandt had another nickname too. It seems that he had a pronounced liking for various shades of blue cloth. Purchasing a full bolt, he'd have all his clothes, including Sunday-go-to-meeting suits, made up from it. This led to the farmer-mechanic-bridge builder being dubbed "Blue Jeans."

Between 1865 and 1872 Brandt employed young James W. Buchanan of Basil as his foreman. After working long summers on the bridges, Buchanan taught school the rest of the year. Most of the bridges on which he labored were local ones, with the exception of a season when Blue Jeans took a contract for some trusswork near DeGraff in Logan County.

In business for himself in the 1890's James Buchanan continued the reputation for good bridges established by Cap Brandt, though he made more of a practice of preparing his timbers directly at the bridge site. Northwestern University professor J. W. Buchanan, son of the builder, vividly recalled eight summers that he worked for his father at bridge fabrication and erection in Ohio. His account also gives an insight into the methods used and tools involved:

52. *Eldorado Road Bridge south of Gettysburg, Ohio, (1891–1958).*

53. *Brubaker Bridge built by Evrett Sherman over Sam's Run near Gratis, Ohio.*

54. *Interior of Brubaker Bridge, built in 1887, with odd empty center panel of Childs truss design.*

Framing was usually done along the road adjacent to the bridge, and generally the site was down in a valley where no breeze ever seemed to reach you. The lower chords were made of freshly-sawed green white-oak, 6 × 14 inches, tremendously heavy and as long as the original tree would permit. These were hauled to the bridge sites on long-coupled wagons and handled with cant-hooks and crowbars. Splice hooks were framed at the ends by scoring with a crosscut saw and foot adze. Daps [notches] were also cut at proper intervals for fitting the bases of the upright posts. All mortises were made by boring four holes about 5″ to 6″ deep and then squared out with mallet and chisels. My back still aches from sitting on the seat of a boring machine, turning the 2-inch bit into that green oak.

55. *Christman Bridge northwest of Eaton, Ohio, still has stencilled name of timber dealer on interior beams.*

After the members of each chord were thus prepared, they were additionally bored through the splices with an extended ⅝-inch bit and ordinary brace. That too brought out the perspiration!

If possible, the floor of the old bridge was shored up and braced to be used as a platform on which the new bridge was set up. Otherwise a jerry-built platform was juggled into position with the aid of a winch (and pinched fingers). The frame was assembled on this and once the bridge was "raised" the work reverted to straight carpentry with conventional siding, flooring and roofing.

Employing only hand tools, it generally took six men five to six weeks to frame, erect and finish a 60-foot span. We worked a 10-hour day, 5½ days a week. After a summer of this work, one became as hard and tough as the oak timbers in the bridges.

My father put camber in bridges by driving wedges behind each brace. It was done with great care and many careful measurements, and when finished the bridge was tuned like a violin string. It was part of our duties to inspect and adjust bridges. After a year or so, when the green timber had seasoned, we returned and re-tuned the bridge. If properly framed, the camber was retained with but little sag, even after many years.

That James Buchanan and his son built well is shown by the fact that at least three of their bridges still do duty in the northwestern part of

56. *Former Ashtabula Gulf Bridge, southeast of Ashtabula, Ohio, replaced in 1948.*

57. *Former Collander Road Bridge southeast of Rock Creek, Ohio. Area inundated by new reservoir and bridge burned.*

58. *Stripped of siding in 1949, Ashtabula County's Furnace Road Bridge shows Howe truss construction.*

59. *Mechanicsville Bridge in Ashtabula County is a unique 154' single-span combining Howe plan with arch.*

60. *Oldest of Ashtabula County covered bridges is on Foreman Road at Eagleville.*

61. *Now abandoned, Fobes Road Bridge over Grand River served another Ashtabula County site until flood of 1913.*

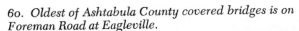

62. *236-foot Harpersfield Bridge is today the longest covered bridge in the state of Ohio.*

63. *Wiswell Road Bridge at Windsor Mills spans deep gorge of Phelps Creek.*

64. *Graham Road Bridge over the Ashtabula River was built after the great flood of 1913.*

65. *Howe truss bridge on Middle Road east of Farnham, Ohio.*

66. *Ashtabula River Bridge between Sheffield Center and Monroe Center, Ohio.*

67. *Former twin covered bridges over Conneaut Creek at Farnham, Ohio.*

68. *Former double-barrel, twin-sidewalked village bridge stood at Newton Falls, Ohio.*

Fairfield County. Their concern with "tuning" the wooden spans is notable. Other less conscientious builders were content to call a job a job and never go back. Over the years maintenance crews have ignored this tricky chore, and gradually it has been forgotten that there ever was a need for it. It is a tribute to both the original builders and to the ruggedness of their wooden framing that so many spans still dot Ohio's countryside.

Despite wholesale losses in recent years, the Buckeye State still has much to offer today's covered-bridge fancier. Roofed spans are to be found in both predictable and unexpected settings in some forty counties, spotted in oddly placed concentrations across the state.

At the extreme northeast corner of Ohio is Ashtabula County, long a covered-bridge stronghold, and still clinging to over a dozen. Readily

70. *Typical neatly arched portals grace one of three spans near Hanoverton in Columbiana County, Ohio.*

reached from I 90 is the Harpersfield Bridge over Grand River. Bypassed but retained and restored, this two-span, 236-foot Howe-truss structure is now the longest in the state. Upstream stands Mechanicsville Bridge, whose 154-foot single span is a unique combination of the Howe plan with an integrated arch. Most of Ashtabula County's bridges follow Ithiel Town's "mode" of construction. One of the most attractive is a weatherbeaten old lattice which perches high on stone abutments and piers over Phelps Creek at Windsor Mills.

To the south is Newton Falls in Trumbull County, site of Ohio's only covered bridge with an attached outside sidewalk. An old lattice bridge, reputedly dating from the 1830's, this

69. *Existing Mahoning River Bridge at Newton Falls retains single sidewalk for pedestrians.*

one spans the East Branch of the Mahoning River.

In Columbiana County, which borders both West Virginia and Pennsylvania, there are records of the former existence of nearly a hundred covered bridges. Today there are six, all little kingpost jobs over streams in the valleys of Little Beaver Creek. Northeast of Lisbon stands a diminutive bridge on Church Hill Road. Though now bypassed, its 19'3" span makes this Ohio's shortest of public-highway bridges.

Representation in the balance of northern Ohio is sparse, with long miles separating existing bridge sites. Preserved in Sandusky County is the old Mull Road Bridge over Wolf Creek southwest of Fremont. Two counties south, the Sandusky River is spanned by a pair of neat Howe-truss bridges, cared for by Wyandot County's Highway Department. Over in Rich-

71. *Little Columbiana County covered bridge north of Lisbon, Ohio.*

72. *Smith truss span south of Rome is Richland County's lone covered bridge specimen.*

land County is the single survivor of a number of Smith patent bridges built in the area during the 1860's and '70's. A single span with black-and-white striped warning paint on the portals, it stands a mile south of Rome.

Also of Smith truss construction is Summit County's lone covered bridge, at Everett over Furnace Run in the valley of the Cuyahoga River. This neat and well-kept span has the further attraction of being the closest covered bridge to the Cleveland metropolitan area.

Trending southward, Harrison County as late as 1930 had fifty-five small covered bridges scattered over all but one of its fifteen townships. Now the region is reduced to a single span on a public highway, and one abandoned bridge on a road leading to some strip-mining property.

73. *Country bridge spans west fork of Little Beaver Creek in Columbiana County, Ohio.*

74. *Mull Road Bridge over Wolf Creek in Sandusky County, Ohio, is sole area survivor.*

Guernsey County has not fared much better, with its handful of weather-worn bridges all dilapidated and neglected. Largely rural, Noble County once had over eighty covered bridges, little locally-built jobs over a host of back-country creeks and runs. Many of them bore the names of men who owned adjacent farms, such as George Gibson, Shad Miller, Dutch Thomas and Pat Bates. Natural features gave nomenclature to others like Road Fork Bridge, Wolf Pen Bridge and Otter Slide Bridge.

The building of Seneca Lake reservoir wiped out a number of Noble's covered crossings, and the ravages of time and progress have today reduced the county's total to eleven.

Closer to the Ohio River, with the larger streams that feed it, lies Washington County. Interest generated in the historically minded old

75. *Furnace Run Bridge at Everett in Summit County, Ohio, bears date of earlier bridge on same site.*

city of Marietta has helped to stem the tide of replacements which for a time threatened to leave the area as covered-bridgeless as Meigs and Gallia counties farther down the river. A dozen remain today, both little bridges and big ones. Adjacent to a 25-mile stretch of Ohio Route 26 northeast of Marietta are four sizable crossings of the Little Muskingum River. Devotees of engineering history will find these

76. *Southeast of Scio, Ohio, a small structure once bridged a diverted creek between major railroad crossings.*

77. *Skull Creek Bridge south of Freeport is Harrison County, Ohio's, last public highway covered span.*

Some former spans in Noble County, Ohio.

78a. *Ashton Bridge, southeast of Caldwell.*

78c. *Glady Creek Bridge.*   78b. *Dutch Thomas Bridge.*

78d. *Jesse Johnson Bridge.*

78e. *John Stephens Bridge.*   78f. *Mud Run Bridge.*

79. Raccoon Creek Bridge on St. 775 in Gallia County, Ohio, combined both regular and suspension arches of Col. Long's 1858 patent.

80. Ohio valley countryside surrounds former Gallia County span over Sunday Creek.

bridges a quick field sampling of forty years of truss development. Represented are Buckingham, Howe and Smith-patent types.

All across southern Ohio historical markers tell of the unexpected presence of Confederate raiders in the state a century ago. Led by the redoubtable John Hunt Morgan, some 2460 guerrillas came up from Sparta, Tennessee and laid waste the Union defenses of Kentucky in the summer of 1863. Plunging north, they boldly crossed the Ohio River west of Louisville and went pillaging across the quiet farmlands. Leaving an arc of destruction in southern Indiana, the Morgan forces entered Ohio at Harrison, to the northwest of Cincinnati.

One of General Morgan's chief objectives was the destruction of enemy property, primarily railroads and communications lines. Covered bridges on both rail lines and highways were vulnerable targets. The guerrillas' speediest method of bridge destruction was to dump a load of hay in a span and set it afire. As it turned out, news of the Confederates' progress across the two states soon put Union troops, local militia and armed citizens in the field to oppose, harass and pursue the invaders. At many sites the Morgan men were too hotly chased to have time to burn their bridges behind them.

81. Former Rulaville Bridge in Gallia County, Ohio, also used inverted arch.

82. Former Long truss with wooden suspension arch at Garner's Ford, Ohio.

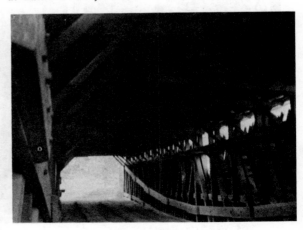

WASHINGTON COUNTY, OHIO --- HISTORIC COVERED BRIDGES ---SERIES NO. 2
PHOTOGRAPHY AND INFORMATION BY S. DURWARD HOAG, HOTEL LAFAYETTE, MARIETTA, OHIO

Marietta, Ohio, October 1953. Washington County has 24 Historic Covered Bridges which are designated by name and number on the County Engineer's Covered Bridge Map. This second series of six Washington County Covered Bridges lists their locations, numbers, names and the streams they cross. Series No. 3 and 4 will be issued before the end of the year.

NO. 1   The RANSOM LANE Bridge, Wesley Twp. W. of Dale, crosses West Branch Wolf Creek.
NO. 6   The HENRY Bridge, Fairfield Twp. N. of Cutler, crosses West Branch Hocking Creek.
NO. 9   The WILLIAMS Bridge, Decatur Twp. W. of Fillmore, crosses West Branch Hocking Creek.
NO. 11   The HARRA Bridge, Watertown Twp. N. W. of Watertown, crosses South Branch Wolf Creek.
NO. 15   The NEEDHAM Bridge(Do not confuse with Needham Bridge No. 14) Dunham Twp. S. W. of Dunham, crosses Little Hocking River.
NO. 16   The CASSADY Bridge, Dunham Twp. S. W. of Dunham, crosses Little Hocking River.

WASHINGTON COUNTY, OHIO --- HISTORIC COVERED BRIDGES --- SERIES NO. 1
PHOTOGRAPHY AND INFORMATION BY S. DURWARD HOAG, HOTEL LAFAYETTE, MARIETTA, OHIO

Marietta, Ohio, October 1953. Washington County has 24 Historic Covered Bridges which are designated by name and number on the County Engineer's Covered Bridge Map. There are approximately 350 Covered Bridges in Ohio, and in 1954, Washington County will rank second with 24. No. 1 Series with the first six Washington County Bridges is listed below with their locations, numbers, names and the streams they cross. Subsequent issues of six bridges each will be published late in 1953.

No. 28   The RINARD Bridge, Ludlow Twp. Near Wingett Run, off St. Rt. 26, crosses Little Muskingum.
No. 3   The SHINN Bridge, Palmer Twp. N. E. of Patten Mills, crosses West Fork Wolf Creek.
No. 8   The ROOT Bridge, Decatur Twp. N. from St. Rt. 555, Crosses West Fork Little Hocking River.
No. 14   The NEEDHAM Bridge, Durham Twp. 3 mi. E. from Veto, crosses Little Hocking River.
No. 13   The ORMISTON Bridge, Barlow Twp. 3 mi. N. Fleming US 50A, crosses Wolf Creek.
No. 7   The DUNBAR Bridge, Fairfield Twp. 1 mi. N. Dunham, crosses Little Hocking Creek.

WASHINGTON COUNTY, OHIO --- HISTORIC COVERED BRIDGES ---SERIES NO. 3
PHOTOGRAPHY AND INFORMATION BY. S. DURWARD HOAG, HOTEL LAFAYETTE, MARIETTA, OHIO

Marietta, Ohio, October 1953. Washington County has 24 Historic Covered Bridges which are designated by name and number on the County Engineer's Covered Bridge Map. This third series of six Washington County Covered Bridges lists below their numbers, names, locations and the streams they cross. The final series No. 4 will be issued in November, 1953.

NO. 4   The LAUREL Bridge (abandoned) Wesley Twp. S. E. of Patten Mills, crosses Laurel Run.
NO. 5   The MALE Bridge, Palmer Twp. S. of Brown's Mill, crosses Southwest Fork Wolf Creek.
NO. 12   The BELL Bridge, Barlow Twp. N. W. of Barlow, crosses Southwest Fork Wolf Creek.
NO. 17   The MILL BRANCH Bridge, Belpre Twp. N. of Porterfield, crosses Little Hocking River.
NO. 18   The HOPKINS Bridge, Dunham Twp. W. of Constitution, crosses East Branch Little Hocking River.
NO. 20   The SCHWENDERMAN Bridge, Warren Twp. S. of Churchtown, crosses Half Way Run.

WASHINGTON COUNTY, OHIO --- HISTORIC COVERED BRIDGES --- SERIES NO. 4(FINAL)
PHOTOGRAPHY AND INFORMATION BY S. DURWARD HOAG, HOTEL LAFAYETTE, MARIETTA, OHIO

Marietta, Ohio, November 1953. Washington County has 24 Historic Covered Bridges which are designated by name and number on the County Engineer's Covered Bridge Map. This last series of 6 Washington County Covered Bridges lists below their numbers, names, locations, and the streams they cross.

No. 21   The HUCK Bridge, Adams Twp. S. W. of Lowell, crosses Rainbow Creek.
No. 22   The FULTON Bridge, Salem Twp. N. E. of Whipple, crosses Paw Paw Creek.
No. 24   The HILDRETH Bridge, Newport Twp. S. of Hills P. O. Rt. 26, crosses Little Muskingum River.
No. 25   The COW RUN Bridge, Lawrence Twp. S. of Sitka, Rt. 26, crosses Little Muskingum River.
No. 27   The HUNE Bridge, Lawrence Twp. S. W. of Lawrence, Rt. 26, crosses Little Muskingum River.
No. 29   The BAKER Bridge, Grandview Twp. N. W. of Dawes on Rt. 7, crosses Leith Run.

Living off the land, the raiders took horses, food and supplies wherever they could find them. The cry of "Morgan is coming!" brought anxiety and fear to little Ohio farms and villages hitherto untouched by war. Men who had never thought about "jining up" grabbed old muskets to help repel the Confederates.

Avoiding large cities, Morgan's route cut a zigzag swath clear across the hilly southern tier of Ohio counties. When Union pincer movements nearly trapped him he kept feinting toward the river in an attempt to get back into friendly territory and join up with General Lee in Virginia.

Three former Guernsey County Bridges—and a survivor.

84a. *Kennedy Bridge southwest of North Salem.*

84b. *Gunn Bridge east of North Salem.*

84c. *Leeper Bridge south of North Salem.*

84d. *Indian Camp Bridge, still standing south of Birds Run.*

A few of the covered bridges burned by Morgan are recorded. One stood over the Ohio Brush Creek at Dunkinsville in Adams County. To the east, the raiders had to effect a crossing of the Scioto at some point. They were rumored to be heading for Chillicothe.

The Chillicothe home guards apprehensively

stationed themselves at the Paint Creek covered bridge south of town. Presently some local scouting parties, out looking for Morgan, were mistaken for the genuine article. In the confusion the guards excitedly burned down the bridge. It was later caustically noted that Paint Creek, bone dry in the summer's heat, contained

85. *Miss Flossie Jones, a WPA travelling librarian, starts out to visit the remote hollows of rural Adams County, Ohio, in the 1930's.*

86. *Cox Bridge, north of Creola in Vinton County, Ohio.*

scarcely a foot of water at the time.

After a battle at Buffington Island on the Ohio River, Morgan's tired and decimated forces turned north again, crossed the Muskingum above McConnelsville and rode through Guernsey County. Passing Point Pleasant, the raiders set fire to a covered bridge over Seneca Creek from which the militia had prudently removed the floor. After they were gone the fire was put out. More success was met at Campbell's Station (now Lore City), where a bridge over Leatherwood Creek went up in flames.

Surrounded, and with their number reduced to only 335 men, Morgan's band burned their last bridge at Nebo (now Bergholz) in Jefferson County on July 25. The next day they finally

surrendered at a spot along the West Fork of Little Beaver Creek near West Point.

For a hundred years, many a roofed and weatherboarded span in southern Ohio was pointed out as "the bridge Morgan tried to burn." Even today, structures no little distance from the Southern raider's actual route are solemnly described as "the bridge Morgan would have burned if he'd decided to come this way." A true war victim, the bridge at Nebo was immediately rebuilt. For decades even its successor was always known as "Morgan Burnt Bridge."

After the dangers of hostile bridge destruction were over, southern Ohio experienced a rash of new building. In Vinton County is Geer's Mill Bridge over Raccoon Creek southwest of Wilkesville. A well-framed Burr arch truss, this one has a pronounced camber of some nineteen inches in both top and bottom chords. Naturally

87. *Pre-U.S. #50 bridge once served tiny rural village of Allenville in Vinton County, Ohio.*

88. *Flat-topped town lattice bridge north of Creola was one of the last to be built new in Ohio, stood from 1918 to 1955.*

89. *"Humpback" or Geers Mill Bridge in Vinton County, Ohio, an unusual Burr truss with arched upper and lower chords.*

known as "The Humpback," the bridge was erected in 1874 by Martin E. McGrath and Lyman Wells. Other Ohio bridges in Coshocton, Perry and Fairfield counties have noticeable "humps" but none arches high above the stream like that of Geer's Mill.

All of Jackson County's covered bridges are on Robert Smith's patent plan, including one built to serve the massive old Buckeye Iron Furnace, now a State Historical Site. Another Smith bridge at Otway in Scioto County has been

bypassed, but is kept in trim by a locally organized community association.

In Lawrence County stands the southernmost covered bridge in Ohio. Nestled below a hillside, this one appears from a distance to be a conventional wooden structure. Closer inspection discloses the queenpost frame to be of iron pipe, and the roof and siding of galvanized iron sheets. Though somewhat similar "iron covered bridges" stand in Alabama and Oregon, this construction is a decided novelty for Ohio.

90. *Interior of Geers Mill Bridge shows pronounced camber of roadway which results in humpbacked appearance.*

91. *Otway Bridge in Scioto County, Ohio, has been by-passed but is preserved by community effort.*

92. *Guyan Creek Bridge in Ohio's Lawrence County is framed with galvanized iron pipe, is state's southernmost covered span.*

93. *"Warren" truss of Mud Lick Creek Bridge south of Germantown, Ohio, as it appeared with arch at former location on Jasper Road in Greene County.*

When it came to using iron, the rods in "combination" bridges such as the Howe truss were very common. But only in Ohio did any builder devise a combination wood-and-iron suspension bridge, and top it with a wooden roof.

Such a fabrication carries East Center Street across Little Twin Creek in Germantown, Montgomery County. Sometimes called an "inverted metal bowstring," this unusual 103-foot bridge was originally built in 1870 on the Old Dayton Pike nearby. Its hanging bowstring consists of two 2 × ½-inch plates, from which ⅝-inch rods are suspended stirrup-fashion to support the floor beams. Moved to its present site in 1911, the bridge never had any siding. In 1964 it was completely restored, painted an attractive white and re-dedicated. Seventy-five per cent of the cost was met by donations from individuals, the various state and national covered bridge societies, and other historically minded groups.

Over on the side of Dayton, Greene County's remaining covered bridges provide a delightful excursion into rural and semirural Ohio. Red-

94. *Unique suspension arch bridge at Germantown, Ohio, was built to serve nearby Dayton Pike in 1870.*

96. *Detail of truss construction used in Germantown's inverted bowstring arch covered bridge.*

95. *103-foot covered inverted iron arch bridge at Germantown after restoration in 1964.*

97. *Ballard Road Bridge northwest of Jamestown. One of Ohio's prettiest covered bridge settings.*

98. *Cemetery Road Bridge over Anderson's Fork in Greene County, Ohio.*

99. *Greene County's long Washington Mill Bridge over Little Miami River, burned in second vandalism attempt in 1968.*

100. *Smith Truss Bridge on Engle Mill Road over Anderson's Fork in Greene County.*

101. *Original "Warren" type truss of Feedwire Road Bridge with no arch, before removal and re-design in Dayton's Carillon Park.*

102. Feedwire Road Bridge at original location near Bellbrook, Ohio, before "restoration."

painted for the most part, they bear small green-and-white signs reading:

PLEASE

HELP PRESERVE

THIS

HISTORIC BRIDGE

Outstanding are a group of three large bridges over Anderson's Fork to the east of Spring Valley, all of different construction, and two within sight of each other. Out of Xenia in another direction is Ballard Road Bridge north of New Jasper, spanning the North Branch of Caesar's Creek in a setting of winding stream and overhanging buckeye trees that delight an artistic eye.

Readily accessible to the thousands who visit Dayton's Carillon Park is a transplanted Greene County covered bridge. This 55-foot span stood for many years on Feedwire Road northwest of Bellbrook, in a pleasant rural site similar to that of Ballard Road. Its construction followed a configuration of elongated triangles generally termed the Warren truss.

When replacement of Feedwire Road Bridge was imminent in 1948, the National Cash Register Company acquired the span and dismantled it. Re-erection was accomplished in the company's Carillon Park adjacent to U.S. 25 just south of Dayton, where the bridge joined other relics of Ohio's past.

103. Feedwire Road Bridge as remodeled and placed over old Miami & Erie Canal bed in Carillon Park south of Dayton, Ohio.

104. *Groff Mill Bridge north of Mount Healthy, Ohio, is closest remaining covered bridge to Cincinnati.*

105. *Massive laminated arches supported former Indian Creek Bridge southwest of Hamilton, Ohio.*

Today the red-painted bridge spans the dry bed of the old Miami and Erie Canal, just east of a restored stone canal lock. To anyone who knew the structure in its original Greene County days, recognition of the covered bridge would be very difficult. Though the work is attractive and commendable, for some reason the little bridge was completely altered. Overhanging portals now protrude on either end, and a pair of fake arches have been unnecessarily added to the trusses.

Closest to Cincinnati, and the only covered bridge remaining in Hamilton County is the little crossing over the West Fork of Mill Creek north of Mt. Healthy. Originally erected in 1850, it served the immense old Groff Mill, which still looms beyond its portal, high on the creek bank. Restoration and continued service of this bridge were ensured by the unobtrusive insertion of steel beams below its flooring.

Mention has already been made of the very

old double-barreled Roberts Bridge south of Eaton in Preble County, as well as the unusual Childs-truss spans erected by Evrett S. Sherman in the same county. Seven of the white-painted Sherman bridges can be found on roads fanning out from Eaton.

106. *Simple queenpost truss supporting Groff Mill Bridge has been augmented by hidden steel beam understructure.*

107. *Interior of lost Straight Creek Bridge shows long trusses with auxiliary arches.*

108. *Brown County, Ohio's, Straight Creek Bridge burned in 1968.*

109. *Eagle Creek Bridge south of Decatur, Ohio, was restored in 1952 after eighty years of service.*

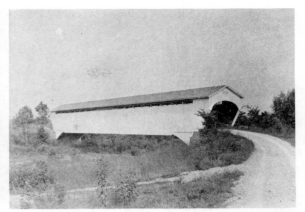

110. *Former long single-span bridge near Seven Mile, Ohio, erected by famed Kennedy family of Indiana.*

Other southwestern Ohio covered bridges include one in Clermont County near Perrintown and Brown County's eight big remaining specimens. Most of these are back from the Ohio River in the Georgetown-Ripley area. To the north, the New Hope-Bethel Road spans White Oak Creek by means of a 162-foot Howe truss which also contains an auxiliary arch. This massive piece of woodwork is composed of eleven thicknesses of laminated plank.

Farther out on the Cincinnati-Dayton perimeter is the bypassed Tallawanda Creek bridge on the outskirts of the university town of Oxford; it is soon to be moved to Hamilton. Shelby County's only covered bridge spans the Great Miami River east of Lockington, a long dark passage reached by auxiliary iron span approaches over the river bottomlands.

Note has been made of the popularity of the Smith-patent truss bridge in Miami County, long the home ground of its inventor, Robert W.

Smith. It is ironic that the county's lone survivor today should be a bridge on Colonel S. H. Long's plan which predates any of the Smith bridges. This is the E. L. Dean Bridge just north of Troy, built in 1860 at a cost of $3,969.68. The second longest in Ohio, it stretches with two solid spans some 223 feet across the Great Miami. Though now bypassed, it is still kept open for passage of the automobiles of occasional visiting admirers.

Farther up the Great Miami, Logan County maintains two sizable Howe-truss bridges, both dating from the 1870 period when Ohio's bridge-building enjoyed such a spurt. Over in Union County can be found the five truss bridges put up by Marysville's inventor-patentee Reuben L. Partridge. White-painted and whitewashed within, they span Big Darby Creek and its tributaries to the south and west of the county seat. The biggest and best one, an ex-state highway bridge off Ohio Route 38, has been bypassed in recent years, but is retained by a locally

111. *Transplanted Tallawanda Creek Bridge north of Oxford, Ohio, has Long truss originally framed for only a single span.*

112. *Shelby County's only remaining covered bridge spans Great Miami River two miles east of Lockington, Ohio.*

113. Licking County covered bridge northeast of Alexandria, Ohio, succumbed to highway improvement in 1965.

114. Typical Licking County covered bridge spans Lobdell Creek southeast of Johnstown, Ohio.

organized group of bridge fanciers. Its attractive setting with trees and sparkling stream makes it a fine memento of Union County's part in the long history of covered-bridge building.

In central Ohio there are still ten little king-post bridges on roads to the north, east and west of Newark in Licking County. A number are painted with black and yellow stripes on the portals, as a warning to oncoming drivers. Perry County's covered spans include the slightly humped bridge which arches over Rush Creek

west of Somerset, and three crossings of a branch of Jonathan Creek to the south of Chalfants. These last were obviously the work of the same builder, and are almost in sight of one another. The "South Bridge" has a neat board-and-batten finish and is embellished with cross-braced gingerbread, topped by a saucy wooden spike which points heavenward from the ridgepole. A fifth covered bridge is located in the extreme northeast corner of Perry County, down in a deep hollow over a pretty stream called Kents Run.

115. South Bridge over a branch of Jonathan Creek near Chalfonts, Ohio, has chapel-like portal.

117. *Remote, yet close to main-travelled highways is bridge over Kents Run northeast of Mt. Perry, Ohio.*

116. *Rush Creek Bridge west of Somerset, Ohio, is built with slightly arched chords.*

119. *Sturdy Long truss bridge over Deer Creek northeast of Greenland, Ohio, was another arson victim of recent years.*

118. *Blairs Bridge over Grand River south of Perry was the last covered bridge in Lake County, stood until 1951.*

121. *Fayette County's last covered bridge, built with these 245-foot two-span Howe trusses, went up in smoke from arsonist's blaze.*

120. *Church Bridge near Chalfonts in Perry County, Ohio.*

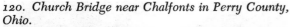

122. *Deer Creek Bridge north of Pancoastburg, Fayette County, Ohio, was state's longest until burned in 1965.*

123. *Last-built of the old-time covered bridges to be built in Ohio was this flat-roofed span near Bremen.*

124. *Rock Mill Bridge northwest of Lancaster is one of Ohio's best-known and most frequently photographed covered bridges. It spans deep gorge of infant Hocking River.*

125. *Builder's sign in former Rush Creek Bridge near Bremen establishes 1920 completion date.*

126. *Unique Jonathan Bright No. 2 Bridge northeast of Carroll, Ohio, contains both an iron suspension arch and a conventional wooden arch.*

127. *Truss of Jonathan Bright No. 2 Bridge discloses details of inverted bowstring probably erected by the Hocking Valley Bridge Works of Lancaster, Ohio.*

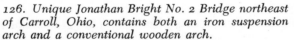

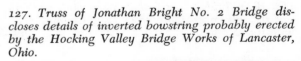

Just a few miles southeast of the capital district of Columbus lies Fairfield County, far and away *the* covered-bridge county of Ohio. Should a casual visitor to the state have time for only a day or two to hunt up covered bridges, he would find in this one county not only a capsule sampling of what the state has to offer, but also a cross-section of adjacent types of Buckeye covered-bridge scenery.

Then too, for the engineering historian or amateur student of truss design, Fairfield County is El Dorado. Here are Burr, Howe and Smith trusses; multiple kingposts, queenposts and a combination of the two. Here are bridges with a hump, built on skews and with added laminated arches. There is even an inverted metal arch, or suspension bridge.

This last, the unique Jonathan Bright No. 2 Bridge, is located northeast of Carroll in Liberty Township. Basically, it is of similar design to the inverted bowstring bridge at Germantown. The Fairfield County example is augmented by additional squared wooden arches, through which the metal plates of the suspension members pass. Nothing quite like it exists anywhere.

Nearby is Jonathan Bright No. 1 Bridge, also an inverted bowstring truss and suspension job, but built entirely of iron plate and columns. No. 1 bears the nameplate of the Hocking Valley Bridge Works of Lancaster, Ohio, whose proprietor was a Benjamin F. Dum. Due to the noticeable similarity between the neighboring structures, Mr. Dum's company is presumed to have had a hand in the erection of the covered bridge in 1881. Perhaps subsequent research will result in naming the type a "Dum bridge."

With good gravel highways, many of them blacktopped, Fairfield also stars as a backroader's paradise in the seeking out of covered bridges. Clear Creek in the southern part of the county flows under five of them in six miles. The first spans are brightly painted in white and dominate the rural flatland. Beyond Clearport the creek dips into a deep valley lined with snake grass and bends around the high limestone bluff of Written Rock. Opposite this huge landmark is a bridge leading to the Sisco farm. Despite the spectacular setting, a chord and arch of the span are broken and sagging. It is being kept in existence only because Clear Creek Valley may

soon become the site of a new reservoir, and replacement would be impractical.

Cruising the low hills nearer the Columbus edge of Fairfield County, bridge after bridge pops into view. These include the Walnut Creek crossings built by Basil's (now Baltimore) famed James W. Buchanan. There are also a number of bridges that were first built over the Ohio & Erie Canal, which have thriftily been moved to new sites. South of this group is scenic Rock Mill Bridge, one of the most photographed of Ohio's roofed spans. This little 33-foot queenpost with open sides is built upon natural rock outcroppings above the infant Hocking River. The gorge here, fifty feet deep, gives the little bridge added fame as one of the highest in the state. In the hillier country of the Rushville-Bremen area are found still another group of Fairfield County's bounteous supply of timbered tunnels. Well-marked maps supplied by the county engineer make it readily possible to drive directly to them all.

How does Fairfield County manage to cling to thirty covered bridges, the second greatest number of any county in the United States? In the first place they were well built. Next, they were well cared for, with county highway officials taking an interest in their retention as an economic saving of public funds. Added to all this, despite obvious obsolescence of the bridges, and the modernization of roads, most Fairfield County people accept and really *like* the bridges. They overlook the sharp-turned entrances, the narrow confines and the occasional "is-this-bridge-really-safe?" feeling. So the bridges stand, for new generations to inherit and perhaps carry on the traditions of maintenance and full use.

As more and more of the spans approach the century mark, the ravages of time, neglect and rampant vandalism will doubtless drastically lower Ohio's grand total of covered bridges. But the picture is not altogether dark. Mention has already been made of a number of the old structures which have been bypassed and preserved. Others have been moved or are soon to be moved to new sites. Hopefully, they will be over some body of water, no matter how small the trickle, since a covered bridge flat on dry land seldom pleases the eye.

A Selection of Fairfield County, Ohio, covered bridges.

128a. *Hannaway Bridge, south of Clearport.*   128b. *Mink Hollow Bridge, northeast of Clearport.*

128c. *Written Rock Bridge, southeast of Clearport.*   128d. *Jonathan Rabb Bridge, northwest of Rush Creek.*   128c. *Johnson Bridge, east of Clearport.*

128f. *E. B. Weaver Bridge, northeast of Carroll.*   128g. *Valentine Bridge, east of Amanda.*   128h. *Shade Bridge, southeast of Canal Winchester.*

128i. *Zeller Smith Bridge, east of Canal Winchester.*

128j. *Macklin House Bridge, northwest of Baltimore.*

128k. *Mary Ruffner Bridge, north of Rushville.*

128l. *Moyer Bridge, northeast of Rush Creek.*

128m. *Shryer Bridge, northwest of Baltimore (built on skew).*

128n. *Taylor Bridge, northeast of Pickerington.*

128o. *Landis School Bridge, southeast of Amanda.*

128p. *Blacklick Bridge, northwest of Pickerington.*

128q. *George Hutchins Bridge, southeast of Amanda.*

129–130. *Last to stand in Mahoning County was a covered bridge southeast of Ellsworth over Meander Creek.*

131. *Ashland County state road bridge once stood near Loudonville, Ohio.*

132. *Parker Bridge northeast of Upper Sandusky is one of two surviving covered spans in Wyandot County.*

133. *West of Chillicothe, Ohio, U.S. #50 formerly used covered bridge to enter village of Bourneville.*

134. *Town lattice bridge north of Adephi, Ohio, stood from 1848 to 1954.*

135. Former state highway covered bridge over Rocky Fork near Hillsboro, Ohio.

136. Well-built double-barrel Town lattice spanned north fork of Paint Creek east of Washington Court House, Ohio.

One of the more unusual solutions to the problem of proper salvation and preservation of a covered bridge was carried out in Muskingum County. This region, once the site of the "Y" and other covered bridges, had had its total reduced in recent years to two. One was an abandoned structure spanning Salt Creek northwest of Norwich. Built in 1870, the 87-foot span was on the

137. Salt Creek Bridge in Muskingum County is owned and maintained by the Southern Ohio Covered Bridge Association. This view shows it when part of public road.

rare Warren plan of truss construction. After being bypassed by a new county bridge, the older crossing reverted to the private owners of the adjacent property, and was occasionally used for the storage of machinery.

In 1960, the Southern Ohio Covered Bridge Association was organized in Zanesville. One of the first acts of the new group was to actually buy the Salt Creek Bridge. Scoffers and killjoys jeered: "What will you do with an old bridge 'way out in the sticks like that?"

Unheeding, the committee went ahead and clinched a deal: $300 to owner Richard Wise for the bridge and two-thirds of an acre of ground. The association members, with donations to buy tin sheets, put in their own time and labor to give their acquisition a new roof. By Sunday, October 21, 1962, old Salt Creek Bridge was ready for rededication as "A Memorial to Early Bridge Construction in Ohio."

Since that time, SOCBA officers and members have kept their unusual Warren-truss bridge in good repair, and find that it makes a dandy place in which to hold the association's outings. Even a shower cannot spoil a picnic-meeting, with the bridge to retire to. Both charter members and recent joiners of the Southern Ohio Covered Bridge Association, with a real bridge to care for, feel that they have a personal stake in the often battered and buffeted cause of covered-bridge preservation.

III

INDIANA
Pride of Hoosiers

A BRIEF study of a relief map of Indiana will show why this state has long been a stronghold of the covered bridge. The Wabash River and its tributaries flow generally southwestward into the broadening Ohio, all fed by lesser streams with descriptive names like Flat Rock, Wildcat, Eel and Raccoon.

There are rivers in profusion, but they seldom tumble madly along on their journeys. Instead they wind mysteriously through farmland and past the cities of the Hoosier State, contained (in most seasons) well within their scoured, rounded channels. A typical Indiana river is only briefly seen at the moment of crossing. Its existence is more noticeable as an elongated tangle of sycamores, poplars and underbrush which line steep clay banks and go snaking off on a quickly undefinable course.

These many rivers and the wealth of good workable virgin timber surrounding them made the use of wood for building bridges preordained. Again it was the presence of knowledgeable men at the right place and time to overcome nature's obstacles by using her gifts. Indiana saw the building of some of America's finest covered bridges.

During the first years of statehood, travel in Indiana was confined to old trails and "traces" which were often just that and nothing more. The primitive horseback routes filtered through the woods and required long detours to reach places where a stream could be forded.

Soon the political rallying cry in the Middle West was "Internal Improvements!" In Hoosierdom it resulted in a rash of canal, road and bridge construction in the early 1830's. Like an arrow driven into the state from the east, the Federal Government's National Road pierced

straight toward the newly built capital city of Indianapolis. As in Ohio, its influence on emigration and commerce was enormous, even though the effect was somewhat blunted by the fact that the road took more than a decade to build. A

138. *Sugar Creek Bridge at Darlington, Indiana, has seen a century of service.*

139. *Main Street Bridge at Richmond, Indiana, was built on wool sack foundations; became a giant bill board.*

140. One of a pair of lattice bridges built under personal supervision of inventor Ithiel Town over Wabash River at Logansport, Indiana, in 1837.

state-sponsored route from Lake Michigan to the capital was laid out at the same time, as well as various privately financed turnpikes in southern Indiana.

When it came to spanning rivers and streams, contracts were let in a number of sections of the state, and several covered bridges were under construction simultaneously. During the period 1831–37 at least six of them were erected on the National Road, and a pair were thrown across the Wabash at Logansport. Perhaps built even earlier was a double-lane crossing of Little Indian Creek on the Paoli Pike out of New Albany, and a twin bridge on the same road east of Greenville.

Due to its size, the honor of being Indiana's first covered bridge appears to have fallen to a little National Road span in Henry County which crossed Symons Creek about three miles east of Straughn. Only 49 feet long, this bridge was of simple queenpost construction, with a

third truss in the middle to divide the lanes of expected traffic. It was completed in the summer of 1834.

The legislators who slogged their way to Indianapolis each year wanted something substantial and ornate for their new capital city's crossing of the White River. The government contract for the National Road bridge here went to Lewis Wernwag, already noted in eastern and adjacent states for his extremely well-built structures. Far removed from his home base in Harpers Ferry, Virginia, Wernwag secured the job at Indianapolis in 1831. He probably drew up plans for it, but gave the actual work to two of his sons, William and Lewis, Jr.

William, with a new partner, William Blake, ran into the problem of "tight money," and the bridge was not complete until 1835. The expenditure of much labor and some $18,000 in cash produced a notable example of the Wernwag talents. Low and wide, the two-span bridge used the designer's special "flared post" and arch construction. It was lavishly finished, with twin covered walkways and colonnaded entrances.

Unhappily, with the passage of years the grand bridge became a victim of neglect. Unsavory characters and footpads lounged in the pedestrian passages so that they had to be barricaded. Buffeted by countless wagons for seventy-two years, the ornate entrance posts were reduced to splintered stumps. A last indignity was the use of the structure for advertising, with signs extolling the virtues of Colgan's Balsam Gum, Senate Twist Tobacco, and Columbus Buggys tacked, painted and plastered higgledy-piggledy from end to end both inside and out.

Another landmark bridge of the National Road stood at Richmond, spanning the East Fork of Whitewater River at the foot of Main Street. This too was a double-tunnel structure, mounted on high and massive stonework abutments and carrying twin arcaded sidewalks which originally were protected with covering and shuttered windows of their own. While not credited to him, the Wernwag flair for heavy timbering and perfectly joined arches was evident in the construction, which was finished in 1835. A quick-

sand condition at the site is said to have been remedied by the sinking of hundreds of sacks of wool below the subfoundation.

Almost as long lived, the Richmond Bridge had a history similar to its Indianapolis counterpart farther out the National Road. Though not as battered and tattered as the latter, it also became an eyesore of miscellaneous advertising. Local merchants proclaimed their wares all over it. Ellwood Morris hawked "Wall Paper, Books, Art and Fancy Goods" on the abutments and stone parapets, while George H. Knollenberg's choice spot for "Dry Goods and Carpets" was the old shingled roof.

Farther north in Indiana, a company was formed in 1835 to erect a bridge over the Wabash at Logansport. Apparently this actually consisted of two bridges, bisected in midchannel by Biddle's Island. The directors of the enterprise secured the services of no less a bridge promoter than Ithiel Town to draw plans for their bold structures.

Mr. Town happened to be in the state at the time on an architectural mission, the design of the first state capitol building at Indianapolis. As always, he was on the lookout for the sale of

141. Artist's conception of small National Road bridge over Pogue's Run. Site is now in urban Indianapolis.

142. *National Road Bridge over White River at Indianapolis designed by Lewis Wernwag, it was completed in 1835 and served until 1907.*

rights to his patent lattice bridge, and seized the opportunity offered at Logansport. In company with two partners named Livermore and Peck, Town even contracted to actually build the bridges during his Middle Western stay, completing them in 1837.

Next to peddle bridge patent rights in Indiana were Colonel Stephen H. Long and his brother Moses, operating by mail from New Hampshire and later Rochester, New York. With the distances involved and slow mail service, most of their business negotiations were arranged by locally appointed lawyers and other men of substance. In Hoosier country these subagents met with little success, and only a few Long-truss bridges were built in the state. There were at least two on the National Road in Wayne County, and in 1840 James Morris undertook to erect one of the type over the East Fork of the Whitewater at Brownsville in Union County. Partially boxed in, this venerable span is today the oldest covered bridge in Indiana still standing at its original site.

Another brother of the bridge-inventing colonel was George Washington Long, also an army officer. He too patented a wooden truss bridge on March 10, 1830, only four days after the

better known design of Colonel Stephen Long received official sanction. George's bridge appears to have been an all-wooden bowstring arch, termed by the patentee an "Elliptical Frame Bridge."

Busy on construction of coastal forts at the mouth of the Mississippi River, George Long was unable to give much time or thought to the marketing of his patent truss. In 1831 he gave the use of the design for the building of a bridge over Tanner's Creek near Lawrenceburg, Indiana. This experimental job was erected by

143. *Oldest Indiana covered bridge still on its original site, at Brownsville. Also only Long truss in state.*

144. Wabash River covered bridge for the National Road at Terre Haute, completed in 1864 by Indiana builder Joseph J. Daniels.

Jonathan Woodbury, with the 400-foot structure mostly on bents forty feet apart and fifty feet above the creek bed. The main span, on "Long's Elliptical Frame" plan, was 76 feet long. Whether or not it was covered is not mentioned. Writing in 1835, George Washington Long mentioned that "others were now building in the same neighborhood," but the Lawrenceburg crossing is the only example of the type known to have existed.

Nearby, on Main Street in Aurora, George W. Lane erected a big solid covered bridge over

145. St. Mary's River Aqueduct of the Wabash & Erie Canal sheltered three decades of Fort Wayne skinny-dippers.

Hogan Creek in 1836, which stood until 1887. This well-traveled region of southeastern Indiana was long a proving ground for other innovations in the wooden-bridge-building world. West of Aurora were the first of the intricate McCallum truss spans in the Midwest, built for the Ohio & Mississippi Railroad. Also reported built at Aurora in 1868 was a Howe-truss bridge of 300-foot single span. Probably a railroad structure, it is a record for this type.

Canals were pushed across Indiana close on the heels of the turnpike roads. Foremost was the Wabash & Erie, which cut diagonally to the southwest from Fort Wayne to Evansville. Threatening the economy of the state during the internal improvements craze, it was haphazardly built in bits and pieces, with "temporary" all-wooden locks and trestle aqueducts that saved the enormous cost and time-consuming labor required for stone structures. Indiana's near bankruptcy in 1834 stopped the work, and much that had been finished began to rot unused in the sunshine and rains.

Reactivated, and financed by the issue of scrip, the canal at last reached Terre Haute in 1849. Along its course were a number of covered bridges, including one with a towpath walkway by which canal boats were hauled across the slackwater of the Wabash River near Carrollton. Above Lafayette a similar "towing path and road bridge" crossed Wild Cat Creek, a 160-foot Long truss built under the direction of the state in 1847.

As in Ohio and Pennsylvania, there were a few covered aqueducts. A small one spanned Big Shawnee Creek below Attica. Best known was that over St. Mary's River in Fort Wayne, which stood about 100 yards north of the present Main Street Bridge. Of two spans, on the Burr-truss plan, the 160-foot aqueduct had its wooden trunk lined with dirt in a vain effort to curb leakage. Built in 1845–46, it became a haven for the youth of Fort Wayne. Many a hot summer afternoon was spent swimming in its cool interior, punctuated by the occasional passage of plodding mules and blunt-nosed canal boats. Blended with the splash of waste water cascading into the St. Mary's were the whoops and hollers of suitless mermen.

The St. Mary's Aqueduct lost its roof in 1872

and ten years later was dynamited out of existence to make way for a railroad bridge. But it was not forgotten. Today a small monument stands in a little park nearby, erected in memory of those boys who once swam beneath the friendly sheltering roof of the old water-filled crossing.

When it came to erecting covered bridges, Indiana not only had ample forests of lumber, but was also blessed with some unusually talented bridge builders. One of the earliest was a man of shadowy history whose working region encompassed the Crawfordsville-Greencastle area. He was Aaron Wolf, who built at least seven covered bridges in three counties during the period 1838–60. Though all seven had notable similarities in timber arrangements, portal design and horizontal finish, only one bears his name, and some of the structures have been attributed to a Henry Wolf, Wolfe, or Woolf.

A pair of spans for the New Albany to Crawfordsville Pike were Wolf's first contribution to Indiana's list of covered bridges. Erected in 1838 were the big double-barreled Burr arch structures across Ramp Creek just south of Fincastle, and over Big Raccoon Creek at the south edge of the village of Raccoon. Though somewhat altered, and on different sites today, these are Indiana's oldest existing covered bridges.

After an unexplained lapse of sixteen years, Aaron Wolf's next recorded bridge was an outstanding 160-foot span over Sugar Creek at Yountsville, west of Crawfordsville. Built with three trusses, this span was a soaring example of the carpenter-contractor's art, a massive, firmly secured arch some forty feet in the air.

Other Wolf bridges included two near Greencastle, one at Portland Mills in Parke County (standing today at Dooley Station in the same county), and a unique span over Little Raccoon Creek east of Rockville. This last featured an eye-catching full half-circle portal, instead of the conventional gable.

Lesser known, since none of his bridges still stand, was Samuel Hege of Columbus. A Pennsylvanian by birth, Hege was raised in Fairfield County, Ohio, and apprenticed at seventeen to a bridge builder in Circleville. For two years he worked for 12½ cents a day. By 1844 he had learned enough to be sent to Harrisburg, Penn-

146. Aaron Wolf's Raccoon Creek Bridge as it appeared for over a century in its original location.

sylvania; he was foreman of a bridge gang at nineteen. The job was to quickly rebuild a 4277-foot Town lattice railroad-highway structure across the Susquehanna River, which had been destroyed by fire. The big bridge was completed in record time with no hitches, and Sam Hege came back to the Middle West as his own man.

Indiana, slowly recovering from financial panic, had just recommenced pushing the Madison & Indianapolis Railroad on through to the capital. Hege was made superintendent in charge of bridge construction from Giffiths (now Queeneville) north, with headquarters in Columbus. In the latter town he was to remain for the rest of his life.

At that date in the early 1840's the railroad presumably required that Hege build the bridges he knew best—Town lattices—and he put up a highway crossing of this type for a toll-bridge company chartered in Columbus. Completed in

147. Converted to single-span, old Raccoon Bridge now bridges Little Walnut Creek south of Clinton Falls.

148. *Ramp Creek Bridge built by Aaron Wolf near Fincastle, in 1838, now serves Brown County State Park; is Indiana's oldest.*

149. *376-foot bridge built over east fork of White River west of Williams, Indiana, by J. J. Daniels.*

1847, this crossing of Driftwood River was Indiana's only known Town patent bridge with the exception of those built at Logansport by the inventor himself.

Joined by his younger brother Levi in 1853, Samuel Hege set up business as a contractor for bridges and other heavy construction. The firm began with three spans built on a rail line projected to avoid the 5.89% grade (steepest on an American Class I railroad) of Madison Hill. Trackless, the bridges over Clifty Creek, along with two tunnels which can be seen today, were part of a $309,000 "improvement" which was never finished. The bridges were probably on the Howe type, as the Hege Brothers soon

joined the parade of builders using the popular plan originally devised for railroads. Before devoting most of their efforts to commercial building, the Heges joined with Adam Keller to put up a good highway version of the Howe bridge over Flat Rock River on Eighth Street in Columbus.

An open-minded man, Samuel Hege switched other things in addition to bridge plans. He is reported to have changed his religion once and his politics twice. A widower for thirteen years, one afternoon in 1863 he told his nearly grown family that he was going to Carthage. They idly

150. *Another Wolf-built covered bridge served Yountsville, Indiana, from 1854 to 1948.*

151. *A Britton-built bridge of 1917 spans Cornstalk Creek near Raccoon in Putnam County, Indiana.*

152. *J. J. Daniels' Jackson Bridge at Rockport is longest single-span covered structure in Indiana; third longest in the nation.*

thought it was perhaps in connection with some bridge contract.

"Yes," continued Hege, "I'm going to Carthage this evening and get married." Departing from his speechless family on the next Shelbyville local, that's just what he did.

Indiana's greatest and most prolific bridge builder was Joseph J. Daniels of Rockville, whom we have previously encountered building Long-truss bridges in southwestern Ohio.

Originally a contract undertaken by his father, the first Daniels-built bridge in Indiana was completed in the summer of 1850. It was located on the first section of the Versailles Turnpike out of Rising Sun. The following year the twenty-five-year-old builder-contractor was called clear across the state to supervise erection of a bridge in Union Township in Parke County. Thus began an association with central-western Indiana which was to continue for the remainder of his life.

Leaving Ohio for good in 1853, young Daniels put up the most important bridge on the Evansville & Crawfordsville (C&EI), the crossing of

153. *Joseph J. Daniels (18261–926), prolific builder builder of Indiana and Ohio covered bridges.*

154. Early Daniels-built covered bridge near Hillsdale in Vermillion County, Indiana.

155. Pine Bluff Bridge over Big Walnut Creek northeast of Bainbridge, Indiana.

the White River at Hazleton, Indiana. This was described as "one of the *very* best bridges in the west." The builder's work earned him the superintendency of the Evansville & Crawfordsville, a post he filled for eight years.

By 1861, J. J. had had enough of railroad operation, and moved from Patoka to Rockville to recommence work as a bridge builder. His very

156. Well-constructed Howe trusses of Pine Bluff Bridge.

first contract turned out to be a span of king-sized proportions. The Parke County commissioners gave him the job of bridging Sugar Creek at the then important trading center of Rockport Mills. Daniels rose to the occasion.

Over the creek at Rockport he flung a covered bridge with double arches for extra strength. Its single span was 200 feet in the clear, the longest wooden covered bridge in Indiana at the time. War had come to the nation, and both President Lincoln and Governor Morton of Indiana sought to promote harmony between political factions. With the example of Andrew Jackson's defiant cry, "The Federal Union, it must and shall be preserved!" Joseph Daniels named his giant span the Jackson Bridge.

It was the beginning of a regained career which made J. J. Daniels Indiana's greatest single builder of covered bridges. For over forty years he was to superintend the erection of them: nearly fifty for a dozen Hoosier counties as well as several railroads.

Of particular note was his 1868 replacement of the "*very* best" White River railroad bridge with an even better one. Built to carry far greater loads than were envisioned when the first crossing was put up fifteen years previously, this was a four-span, 600-foot masterpiece of extremely heavy beams and arches on the Burr plan. During high water in the summer of 1875, trees, houses and a huge sawmill were dashed against it, "with no damage except the loss of a few pieces of siding."

157. *Over Deer Creek near Manhattan, Indiana, is one of Joseph Daniels' Putnam County covered bridges.*

158. *Putnamville, Indiana, had Howe-truss bridge which was burned in 1967.*

Probably the longest Daniels bridge was the double-barreled, six-span crossing at Terre Haute. Built in 1864, it transported the National Road across the Wabash for forty years. At the time of its demolition, J. J. was completing his final bridge contract, the appropriately named Neet Bridge east of Catlin in his adopted home county of Parke.

Giant among Indiana covered bridge builders, J. J. Daniels physically towered over most of his contemporaries as well. He stood well over six feet tall, and backed up his size with firm convictions and positive expression. Faithful, energetic and efficient in his business dealings, one affidavit described him as "of gentlemanly deportment."

The integrity of the man and his work is illuminated by the story of one of his railroad bridges in Parke County, built in 1865. Twenty years later a local man had charge of a freight creeping slowly along the all-but-submerged track between the bridges over Big and Little Raccoon Creeks. An order had been passed up to the train as it chuffed through Rockville depot at midnight.

"Do not cross Big Raccoon Bridge without examination."

As the long, flood-washed tunnel loomed up in the locomotive's headlight, the engineer opened her up.

"Ain't you goin' to stop?" queried the anxious fireman.

The man at the throttle gave him a glance, his face scornful in the glow from the firebox.

"Hell, no," he retorted. "Dan'ls built that bridge. It's safer'n this damn roadbed!"

With his last years spent in Rockville, enjoying the classic literature and history of which he'd always been fond, the old gentleman died in 1916 at the age of ninety.

Aaron Wolf and J. J. Daniels were not alone in giving west-central Indiana an unusual amount of exceptionally well-built covered bridges. Their work was both supplemented and continued by Joseph A. Britton.

An authentic Hoosier, Britton was born in a log cabin three miles east of Rockville in 1838. After learning the carpenter's trade from his father, he overcame his meager schooling with self-study and took up law. Both avocations were interrupted by service in the ranks of the Union Army during the Civil War, and an unpleasant

159. *Brouillettes Creek Bridge near Universal, Indiana.*

160. Lusk Mill or Narrows Bridge over Sugar Creek was first venture of Indiana builder Joseph A. Britton.

confinement in a Confederate prison camp. Finally admitted to the bar, young Britton started a practice at home in Rockville, later transferring his shingle to Lawrence, Kansas.

Writs and torts proved cloying to a man raised to the tune of pounding hammers and rasping saws. Within ten years the erstwhile attorney was back in Indiana, happily employed at carpentry. Soon a contractor on his own, Joseph Britton followed the example of J. J. Daniels and arranged that his first bridge should be at an important site. It was the spectacularly situated span at the old Lusk Mill, bridging the narrows of Sugar Creek. This well-known structure served for years as the south entrance to Turkey Run

161. Well-known Narrows Bridge is now a permanent feature at entrance to Turkey Run State Park.

State Park, and was the first of some forty covered bridges erected during a thirty-three-year period by Joseph Britton and members of his immediate family.

In general, Britton bridges were of shorter span than the lengthy fabrications undertaken by Daniels. A bridge put up by Joseph and his boys Eugene, Charlton and Edgar had a certain homespun quality which blended with the Indiana landscape. He preferred the Burr design, and even his smallest spans contained arches.

While steel and concrete were coming into full use elsewhere, Joseph Britton and his carpenter sons regularly contracted for wooden bridges with the Parke, Vermillion and Putnam county commissioners. After the disastrous 1913 flood, two of their covered jobs replaced iron bridges which had succumbed to high water. The last Britton bridge was erected in 1920 over Little Raccoon Creek near Catlin. By a quirk of fate, the site was just downstream from J. J. Daniels' swan-song bridge of two decades before. And like Mr. Daniels, Joseph Britton lived a long, full life, dying at ninety in 1929.

Over on the other side of the state lived the Kennedy family, some of the finest craftsmen in wood who ever put hand to a covered bridge. Based at Rushville, three generations of Kennedys erected over fifty bridges in Indiana, and their activities extended over a period of nearly as many years.

The business was started by Archibald Mc-Michael Kennedy, a North Carolinan who came to Indiana in 1825 to engage in carpentry and barn-raising. By the 1860's he had settled in Rush County on a 247-acre farm with a fine brick house he had built himself. In 1870 Archibald added the heavy construction of bridges to his woodworking pursuits, assisted by his son Emmett.

Their first contract was for bridging the East Fork of Whitewater River at Dunlapsville in Union County, a two-span job of 300 feet. The fine workmanship that went into the bridge was immediately apparent to anyone who crossed it, and the word soon got around the state that Arch Kennedy and his boys down in Rushville could toss up a top-notch covered bridge.

For a decade the elder Kennedy, assisted by his sons Emmett and Charles, was busy at bridg-

162. A Kennedy covered bridge under construction in 1873 over White River at Martinsville, Indiana.

ing Indiana rivers and creeks. Arch, a large and colorful man, was a great one to secure contracts. Lanky Emmett usually supervised the actual building, with Charles, who later turned to law, attending to the myriad details of dimensions and supply that went into the work.

Convalescing from an illness in 1872, Emmett occupied his time in fashioning a model of a Burr arch truss. Made of bridge timber scraps joined by special tiny bolts from a jeweler, the little span was forty-two inches long, and could be carried conveniently in a case to bridge lettings.

In the 1870's an Indiana county board of commissioners was usually made up of farmers, doctors and businessmen who knew little of engineering or the reading of plans and specifications. The model gave them a concrete notion of how the completed bridge might appear.

Archibald Kennedy was not contented with just the exhibition of the model. His comments on bridges and bridge building were invariably embellished with an endless supply of humorous stories, culminating in a demonstration wherein he placed a book upon the little bridge, and then stood upon it in triumph. The man weighed some 250 pounds.

163. Emmett L. Kennedy (1848–1938) of Rushville, Indiana, holds model of Burr truss type of bridge which three generations of his family built in Indiana and Ohio.

164. *Former covered bridge over Sand Creek near Westport, Indiana, bore Kennedy name and construction patterns.*

165. *Moved here from Rush County, this neat Kennedy covered bridge now graces Fairground Park at Crown Point, Indiana.*

Tall, bony Emmett could give a like performance when the occasion called for it. His father became a state senator and retired in 1883. Then Emmett and Charles formed their own

166. *Circleville Bridge at Rushville, Indiana. This was Archibald Kennedy's last covered bridge.*

partnership, which was continued in later years by Emmett alone.

In great measure, the Kennedys were responsible for the 1880's being the heyday of covered-bridge construction in Indiana. Although they erected a few framed kingpost and Howe trusses, their preference was for the big Burr arch bridges. Among Kennedy "trademarks" were the heavy lateral struts in the top bracing, double-step joints between posts and diagonals and a special splicing clamp for timbers of the lower chords.

The thing that made a bridge instantly identifiable as "a Kennedy" was the unmistakable trim and finish. They were closely sided with horizontal shiplap, a feature which Emmett believed put additional strength in the truss. On the neatly rounded portal openings were corbels extending out from the roofing and embellishments of fancy scrollwork flush on the facing. To this pleasing combination was added a good coat of white lead paint, with the date of erection and the Kennedy name as builders proudly inscribed.

Emmett Kennedy maintained a block-long yard in Rushville, where his bridge timbers were prepared. At first the family used native oak and yellow poplar (tulip), but later found Michigan white pine the best and easiest to prepare for bridges.

Fulfilling contracts across the state, Emmett Kennedy usually had his timbers prefabricated in Rushville and shipped to the various sites.

167. Side view of Circleville Bridge south of Rushville, Indiana. Kennedy installed sidewalk ceilings at his own expense.

168. Circleville Bridge over Flat Rock River on south edge of Rushville, Indiana. View shows original arched portal and arcaded sidewalks with ceilings.

Fifteen to twenty-five workmen, continuously recruited from the ranks of local carpenters, were supervised in effecting the bridge raising and finish by Emmett and two or three key men of the organization.

That they built well is shown by the surviving examples of their craftsmanship; nearly a dozen of their bridges dot Indiana today. Unfortunately,

the most elaborate of Kennedy creations no longer stand. These were their four double-sidewalked "village" bridges, built to grace the cities of Rushville, Connersville and Shelbyville.

The sidewalks were like the long porches of the Victorian era in which they were built, with elaborately turned posts and balustrades. Rendering tight siding unnecessary, they gave a light

169. East Connersville, Indiana, Bridge, built by the Kennedys in 1887 and considered by them "the best of the lot."

170. *Kennedy Family's Vine Street Bridge over Little Blue River in Shelbyville, Indiana, had the ultimate in refinements: a fully boarded-in roadway ceiling.*

and airy aspect to the bridges. The first of these attractive bridges was built in 1881 at East Hill in Rushville, and followed two years later by what was to be Archibald Kennedy's last bridge-building contract, the Circleville Bridge over Flat Rock River at the south edge of town.

Rush County had been good to Arch and his family, and in this prominent landmark he de-

termined to show his appreciation. Original plans for the bridge did not include any ornamentation over and above that which the Kennedys usually affixed. On the Circleville span, Archibald installed tightly boarded arched ceilings above the sidewalks, at his own expense.

This new departure in the finish trim of covered bridges was continued by Emmett Kennedy in the East Connersville Bridge, considered by the family as "the best of the lot." In 1892 Emmett completed the Vine Street Bridge over Little Blue River in Shelbyville. In this one he went even further, and encased the entire upper portion of the roadway tunnel. Perhaps no covered bridge ever built anywhere in the world duplicated this unique feature.

Competition from iron bridge builders forced Emmett Kennedy to turn to house-building and general carpentry after the beautiful Vine Street Bridge was finished. Then in 1913 he was called out of his initial retirement to rebuild a flood-wrecked crossing of the Whitewater near Metamora. With the steel shortage brought on by World War I he shortly found himself back in the bridge business, assisted by two of his own sons, Charles and Karl. This combination erected the big Norris Ford Bridge over the Flat Rock northeast of Rushville in 1916, and a smaller span in Wayne County two years later. Right

171. *Emmett Kennedy was called out of retirement to rebuild flood ravaged crossings of Whitewater River near Brookville in 1914.*

172. *Longwood Bridge, built west of Connersville in 1884, bears the typical Kennedy trademarks, ornate roof brackets and scrollwork, name and date.*

173. *Final Kennedy Bridge was completed near Fountain City, Indiana, in 1918. Era of Kennedy family building covered nearly half a century*

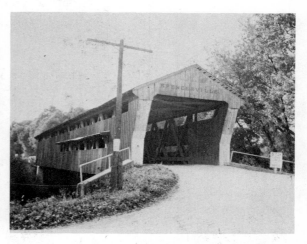

174. *Spencerville Bridge over St. Joseph's River dates from 1875.*

into the 1920's the three Kennedys were kept busy repairing and reconditioning some of the old bridges. And Emmett Kennedy, Indiana's grand old man of covered-bridge building, lived to be ninety, too.

Both J. J. Daniels and the Kennedys could (and did) condescend to build the Howe-truss type of bridge if a county or railroad specifically asked for it. Here and there an occasional Howe span built by local contractors appeared on the Indiana landscape.

Ranging over from Ohio, the Smith Bridge Company of Toledo would put up a good sturdy Howe. They were also responsible for the erection of at least fifteen of their own Smith patent bridges in Indiana, notable examples being at Laketon, Pyrmont and Gosport.

This last, an intercounty crossing, was a three-spanner stretching across the West Fork of White River. Gosport was the locale of a reminiscence by the famed Hoosier poet, James Whitcomb Riley.

It seems that Riley appeared one winter's night at an entertainment in Bloomington. Hoping to catch a train at Gosport he hired a buggy and driver to fetch him the eighteen-odd miles. With every step the vehicle's two little western horses broke through the crust of ice which covered the road, and could only plod along at a walk.

Dawn was breaking when the rig and its weary occupants came in sight of the breakfast smokes of Gosport. Riley puts it:

Well, just as we approached the covered bridge, the driver leaned forward and said, "Mr. Riley, can you see what it says on the end of that bridge?"

"Yes," said I. "It says $5 Fine for Driving through this bridge Faster than a Walk."

He gave the whip just as the hooves of the horses struck the board floor, and brought it down with a switch on the backs of the animals. The horses that had walked all night suddenly leaped into action. It seemed to me we went through that bridge about ninety miles an hour.

"Aha!" shouted the driver. "Here's where I get my Five Dollars' worth!"

175. *North Manchester Bridge over Eel River in Wabash County, Indiana, is a specially-built Smith truss with attached covered sidewalk.*

176. *Cutler Bridge (1876–1952) had customary admonition and offered incentive to informer.*

177. *At Cutler, Indiana, over Wildcat Creek.*

Robert Smith's company that put up the Gosport Bridge in 1870 often had subcontractors who built their type of span on a patent royalty basis. Among these was a builder whose work was predominantly done in the Ohio River valleys of southwestern Indiana, William T. Washer of Cannelton. Washer's earliest spans were a fine application of the Burr arch truss with flared posts, such as had been introduced in the Middle West by the work of Lewis Wernwag. Later, Washer erected at least three bridges in Gibson County on the Smith patent style.

Numerous other Indiana bridge builders did work on far more than just a local scale. These included Josiah Durfee of Noblesville, Philip Ensminger and Thomas A. Hardman of Ripley

178. *South span of Cutler covered bridge with detail of Howe truss plus auxiliary arches.*

County, George Woerntz of Dekalb County and the Western Bridge Works of Fort Wayne.

It is estimated that Indiana once had some four to five hundred covered bridges. The count now is down to an approximate 120 in over thirty counties. The state still offers a goodly number of big, attractive and unique spans for the pleasure and admiration of the visitor.

The northwestern corner of Indiana is watered only by small streams, and much of the region never did have any covered bridges. Archibald Kennedy would be mighty surprised to find a bridge with his name on the portal only forty miles from Chicago, but there it is. Originally built south of Milroy in Rush County, the 85-foot span was disassembled and moved to Crown Point's Fairground Park in 1933. Painted cream, with red trim, it spans a dry depression on a park lane, and is not apt to be threatened by rampaging waters.

Only a few miles north of Fort Wayne are two bridges over St. Joseph River near Spencerville, big white-portaled Howe-truss jobs with red siding, one of which is due for replacement. A third in Dekalb County, recently relocated, gave access to the old Cedar Chapel neighborhood.

At North Manchester in Wabash County is Indiana's only covered bridge with an attached sidewalk on the outside. Painted red with white trim, it is built with a double intersectional system of timbers in a heavy version of the Smith patent. The Smith Bridge Company also has an

179. *Smith Bridge northeast of Rushville, Indiana, has typical horizontal siding as applied by the Kennedy family of bridge builders.*

180. *Former Perkins Corner Bridge west of New Salem, Indiana. A Kennedy bridge in country setting.*

181. *Indiana's own village of Moscow is notable for huge covered bridge built by Emmett Kennedy in 1886.*

182. *Bulk of Moscow Bridge stretches 372 feet in two spans across Big Flat Rock River.*

183. *Forsythe Mill Bridge northeast of Moscow, Indiana, is a long single span built by Emmett Kennedy in 1888.*

184. *Wild Cat Creek Bridge at Owasco, Indiana.*

example of their Howe truss in the board-and-batten-finished Roann Bridge over the same Eel River in the same county. In Kokomo's Highland Park stands the "Vermont Bridge," another Smith patent example which in 1958 was moved four miles from its original site east of the city under the auspices of the Howard County Historical Society and the Kokomo Lions Club.

On down Wild Cat Creek in Carroll County are two bridges dating from the early '70's. That east of Cutler has unusual auxiliary arches added to the Howe trusses, and is mounted on special

185. *Howe truss structure of Owasco, Indiana, bridge.*

186. *Ceylon Bridge over Wabash River northeast of Geneva, Indiana.*

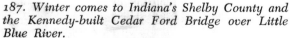

187. *Winter comes to Indiana's Shelby County and the Kennedy-built Cedar Ford Bridge over Little Blue River.*

188. *Lawrence County's lovely bridge at Harrell's Ford was 5 miles north of Bedford.*

cast iron abutments patented by A. Wheelock of Fort Wayne in 1870. Grant County has the "New Cumberland Bridge" east of Mathews. This one was washed away in the flood of 1913, jacked up and returned to its original site on rollers. On up the Wabash is Adams County's Ceylon Bridge northeast of Geneva. And in Randolph County a Kennedy-built bridge can be found over the West Fork of the Mississinewa River, modernized with shiny aluminum siding and roof.

East-central Indiana still clings to some of the beautiful bridges built by the Kennedy clan,

189. Unique Metamora Aqueduct was built for Indiana's Whitewater Canal in 1846.

190. Huge arches supported both trusses and heavy trunk of canal water in original Metamora Aqueduct.

wooden aqueduct, built to carry the oblong trunk of a water-filled canal over the waters of Duck Creek. This structure dates back to 1843 when the Whitewater Canal was dug along the rim of the valley. The original aqueduct, hastily built and not covered, washed out in 1845. It was replaced the following year by a new one, fabricated with framed arches of white oak and white pine, plus a substantial roof. When the canal ceased operation right after the Civil War, a section of the waterway at Metamora was retained to power a local mill. The old aqueduct,

191. Metamora Aqueduct as rebuilt in 1946–49; it is the only covered wooden aqueduct still standing in the United States.

although a number are somewhat battered by time, vandals and ineptly guided trucks. Their first built still straddles the East Fork of Whitewater at Dunlapsville. As might be expected, Rush County's six existing examples are all Kennedy creations, along with the surviving specimens in neighboring Fayette and Shelby counties. Their longest existing covered bridge, a 372-footer, is the main attraction of Indiana's own quiet little village of Moscow.

Of national importance in engineering history is a truly unique bridge at Metamora in Franklin County. This is the world's only known covered

192. Side view of Whitewater Canal Aqueduct at Metamora, Indiana. Excess water drains replace leaky trough.

patched and propped, somehow managed to hold together under its burden of heavy trough and tons of water, though it always leaked like a soap strainer.

After an even century, in 1946, the historical importance of both canal and aqueduct was realized, and steps were taken toward retention and restoration. Acquired by the Whitewater Canal Association and the Indiana Department of Conservation, the old aqueduct was taken apart the same year. Rebuilding took three years, under the able direction of local foreman Donald

E. Bates. Some of the original timbers could be used again, notably the arches and parts which still bore the snubbing marks of canal-boat tow lines. Additional big timbers were obtained from a forest in Kentucky. A new tin roof capped the restored waterway bridge, and a coat of red-brown paint makes the structure appear as though it had always stood exactly with the present appearance. No longer leaky, it contains four baffled holes to purposely drain off excess water into Duck Creek. Along with restored locks and the old mill in Metamora, the prize bridge is

193. Since moved to a park, a Kennedy bridge spanned east fork of Tanner's Creek at Guilford, Indiana.

194. Former Watson-Skeen Bridge near Osgood in Ripley County, Indiana.

195. *Red-painted Busching Bridge over Laughery Creek southeast of Versailles, Indiana.*

196. *Former Indian Lake covered bridge in Marion County, Indiana.*

over Fishback Creek near Traders Point. When replacement time came in 1960 it was moved a short distance to span a pond on the farm of D. W. Brown.

To the south of Indianapolis are two Howe-truss bridges in Jennings County. Two more are in the neighborhood of Columbus: Clifty Creek, moved to a city park, and the Tanney Hill Bridge west of Taylorsville, spanning the Driftwood River.

197. *Former White River Bridge near West Newton was once Indiana's longest. It was Kennedy-built.*

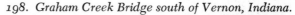

198. *Graham Creek Bridge south of Vernon, Indiana.*

now part of the Whitewater Canal State Memorial.

Confederate raider John Hunt Morgan passed through the Indiana counties of Ripley and Dearborn during his famous raid of 1863, leaving burned bridges in his wake. The Kennedys, Phil Ensminger and Tom Hardman all built covered bridges to replace them in the years that followed, and each has an example still standing in the region.

Indianapolis' county of Marion was once rich in covered timber bridges, but today is reduced to just one, now on private property. This was a Josiah Durfee bridge, originally built in 1882

"Driftwood" was once the name of the entire East Fork of White River, today the locale of Indiana's longest covered bridges. Built by J. J. Daniels are two to the north of Brownstown, and one at Williams, all over 300 feet long. Another Daniels creation at Medora stretches 434 feet in three spans to make it Indiana's longest. Nationally, its length is exceeded only by slightly longer bridges in New Hampshire and the State of Washington.

Well-known, scenic Brown County is today the site of one of the nation's half-dozen remaining two-lane covered bridges. This is the old Ramp Creek Bridge, originally built in 1838 near Fincastle by pioneer bridge architect Aaron Wolf. Bypassed by a new state highway, the double-barreled veteran was moved to a site southeast of Nashville in 1932, where it serves as the northern entrance to Brown County State Park. Though far from its original site, it is the state's oldest covered bridge which retains its first shape and dimensions.

When Monroe Reservoir was cleared and filled in 1965 the Bloomington area lost four of its best covered bridges. More recently Indiana University had thoughts about acquiring a covered

199. *Scipio Bridge in Jennings County, Indiana, is a Howe truss, competently erected by Smith Bridge Company, a rival patent pusher.*

200. *One of J. J. Daniels long bridges over east fork of White River, this one at Brownstown, Indiana.*

201. *Tanney Hill Bridge, West of Taylorsville, Indiana.*

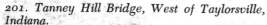

202. *Little Bean Blossom Creek Bridge in Brown County, Indiana, was by-passed and collapsed from neglect.*

203. *Freedom Bridge over West Fork of White River had two spans replaced with a steel arch after 1898 flood. Full replacement came in 1965.*

bridge for its outdoor museum, but it was a bit late for the ones that might have been readily available a few months before. A campaign to obtain a bridge from neighboring Owen County had a good slogan: "Save Freedom (Bridge)!" but practicality dictated the abandonment of the scheme. Freedom Bridge had two spans of 150 feet each, while the River Jordan in Bloomington which it was proposed to span has the width of a good standing broad jump.

Preservation hopes appear brighter for the Bells Ford Bridge northwest of Seymour in Jackson County. Like the Metamora Aqueduct, this bridge is unique in that no other similar structure is known to exist anywhere in the world. Bells Ford is a Post patent truss, built over the East Fork of White River in 1869.

The Post truss was the invention of a New Hampshireman, Simeon S. Post, a man whose other accomplishments include the invention of a parabolic locomotive headlight, the perfection of the original railway telegraph system and the design of the first railway timetable. Invented in 1863, Mr. Post's bridge truss was the outgrowth of many years of study. Known as a "combination truss," since it used fully as much iron as wood, the framing called for main diag-

onals of wood, with a web system of pairs of iron rods for further bracing and counterbracing. The top chords were of wood while the lower ones utilized wrought iron.

Such a bridge was exceedingly intricate to erect, particularly by ordinary bridge carpenters. How such a structure came to be built in south-central Indiana is a mystery, though Mr. Post

204. *Gosport Bridge, half-wood and half-steel, stretched over the west fork of White River until destroyed by arsonists in 1955.*

205. *Bell's Ford Bridge northwest of Seymour, Indiana, over east fork of White River. It is the only known Post patent truss covered bridge in the world.*

206. *Detail of rare truss patented by S. S. Post in 1863; a combination of wood and iron framing. This Indiana one-of-a-kind was built in 1869.*

had formerly been familiar with the region as chief engineer of the Ohio & Mississippi Railroad. Perhaps Bells Ford's builder, Robert Patterson, was a onetime associate of the inventor.

For a decade in the 1870's, the Post truss was popular for both railroad and highway use. Soon built wholly with iron, at least one erected by a company headed by the inventor's son still stands in Massachusetts. But the big 325-foot Indiana specimen is the only known example which incorporates wooden timbers, weatherboarding and a roof. That the unusual design had merit is proved by its continued existence now that the bridge nears the century mark. One of the last covered bridges on an Indiana state highway, it is hoped and planned that Bells Ford may be bypassed and retained for its historical significance in engineering annals.

At least eight covered bridges once served the city of Evansville, but today the whole southwestern section of Indiana retains only six scattered spans. All were erected by the region's best-known builder, William T. Washer, and have the Burr and Smith patent trusses which he favored during his career.

Perhaps the most remote of any covered bridge in Indiana is Washer's old Red Bridge, spanning Big Bayou in the Wabash River bottoms to the southwest of the ghost town of Crawleyville. Three other Washer-built bridges span the Patoka River in Gibson and Pike counties, and two of his earlier ones are over the Anderson

207. *Cade's Mill Bridge over Coal Creek southwest of Veedersburg in Fountain County, Indiana.*

208. *Kennedy-built bridge near Bloomfield, Indiana, over Richland Creek.*

209. *Daniels built this Bridgeton span of 1868 to reach the mill at right.*

River on the Perry-Spencer line. One of the latter has been given an odd appearance. At Huffmans Mills, the Spencer County authorities are reported to have reconditioned their half of

210. *Former Patoka River Bridge northwest of Huntingburg, Dubois County, Indiana.*

the bridge with oil-treated natural redwood siding. Not to be outdone, Perry County restored its half, too, using white paint with green trim!

Any survey of the existing but rapidly diminishing Indiana covered bridges comes to an amazing bright spot in the region to the north and northeast of Terre Haute. Here is found a concentration of over sixty covered bridges. Parke County alone has thirty-six and Putnam twelve.

The well-watered terrain of Parke County, plus long years of contracting by J. J. Daniels, Joseph Britton and others, is responsible for this unusual state of affairs. Other counties have once had as many or more of such landmarks remaining from earlier days. But the people in Parke County did something to preserve and perpetuate their heritage. First formed in 1957, the Parke County Covered Bridge Festival Committee has met with phenomenal success in promoting covered bridges as a tourist attraction.

Sparked by William B. "Billy" Hargrave, editor

211. West Union Bridge over Sugar Creek, Parke County.

of the Rockville *Republican,* and Mrs. Juliet Snowden, the first annual Parke County Covered Bridge Festival got under way in October 1957. It featured free lectures, bus tours, a barbecue chicken dinner and a pancake breakfast. Each visitor was given extensive information about not only the bridges but the entire region, and special easy-to-follow maps were handed the tourist so he need not be afraid of losing his way on the byways of Parke.

Favored with fine fall weather and a good turnout, it was only natural for the committee to say: "Let's do it again!"

The festival is now established as an annual event, a ten-day rural fair with headquarters in a huge tent on Rockville's courthouse square. Thousands of visitors from all over the nation have been attracted to make pilgrimages during the month of flaming leaves, and visit Parke County's covered bridges. With the aid of the annually updated maps they can visit all thirty-six of them, including the famed Jackson Bridge

213. Mansfield Bridge over Parke County's Big Raccoon Creek.

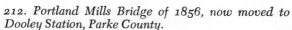
212. Portland Mills Bridge of 1856, now moved to Dooley Station, Parke County.

214. *Cox Ford Bridge, built by Joseph & Edgar Britton.*

215. *Mecca Bridge over Big Raccoon Creek.*

216. *Red Bridge east of Rosedale, over Big Raccoon Creek.*

with its mighty arch, other big Daniels bridges, and those of nearly equally famed Joseph Britton.

The committee has developed quite a paternal feeling toward the bridges. During the decade since the first festival, local interest has been aroused to the point where both hard work and money have been channeled into a preservation program unequaled elsewhere in the United States. Parke County people have now saved and bypassed half a dozen old covered bridges. More than that, through cooperation and effort they have managed to get the Catlin Bridge moved over seven miles to an attractive golf-course setting. And when Dooley Station Bridge was destroyed by arsonists in 1960 they got

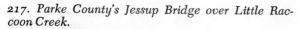

217. *Parke County's Jessup Bridge over Little Raccoon Creek.*

218. *Thorpe Ford Bridge northeast of Rosedale over Big Raccoon Creek.*

Aaron Wolf's old Portland Mills Bridge moved twice as far to take its place. Their 1968 project was the establishment of a covered bridge museum.

Any Hoosier worthy of the name should be proud of the folks down in Parke County. Their success in preserving covered bridges, and in bringing local covered-bridge tours into the eye of the traveling public is to be highly commended, and is already being emulated in other parts of the nation.

219. Nevins Bridge moved to golf course north of Rockeville, Parke County.

220. J. J. Daniels built this double span Burr-truss bridge over Big Raccoon Creek above a mill dam at Bridgeton in famous Parke County.

IV
MICHIGAN
Lumber for All but Their Own

MICHIGAN's lumbermen exported far more native white pine for bridges in other states than they ever used to span local streams. In an economy dependent on the presence or lack of standing timber, both the early settlement in the state and its attendant river crossings were often of a temporary nature.

An example was the Keene Township crossing of Flat River in Ionia County in the center of Michigan. The first bridge there was erected in 1845. It must have been a practical but unpretentious piece of work, for the township road commission gave Ambrose Spencer all of $79.00 to accomplish the job.

By 1856, the crossing had become known as White's Bridge, probably from an immigrant

221. Century-old White's Bridge, near Smyrna, Michigan; built with the rare Brown truss.

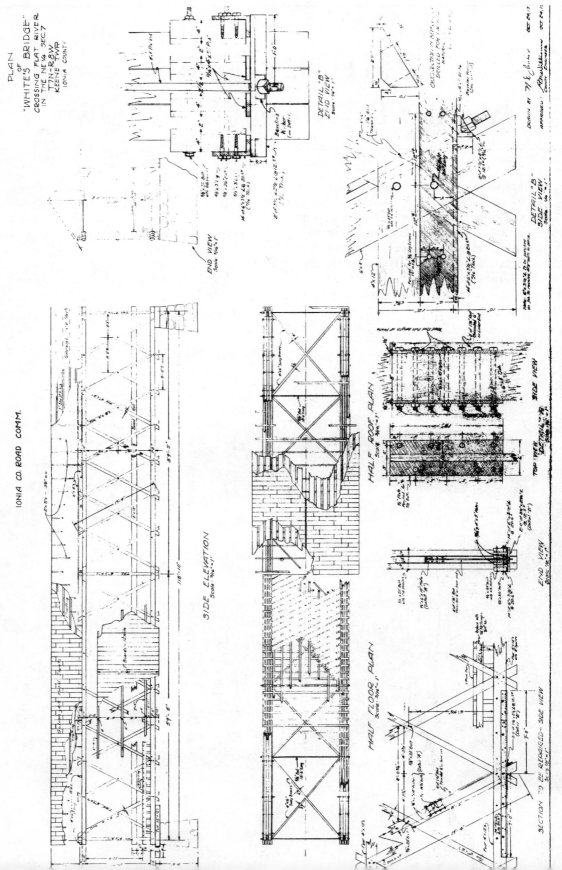

222. *Detailed drawing of White's Bridge.*

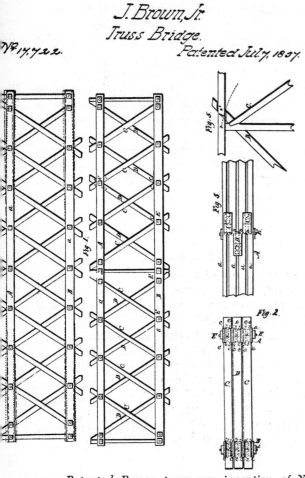

J. Brown, Jr.
Truss Bridge.

Nº 17,722.

Patented Jul. 7, 1857.

223. *Patented Brown truss was invention of York State man, but has been found only in Michigan.*

settler from England named George W. White, who served on the first township road commission. In that year the bridge was replaced, at a still nominal cost of $250.00. When an ice jam in the spring of 1869 took out the second White's Bridge, it was thought to erect something more substantial, even though the town had no means of immediate payment.

Jared N. Brazee and Joseph H. Walker took the contract to complete quickly a 120-foot covered wooden bridge on the site, for a deferred payment of $1000 in 1870 and $700 in 1871. Using timber floated down the Flat River, they had the bridge finished by July 1869. Before approving the project, Keene Township showed further parsimony. Brazee and Walker had apparently used some second-hand lumber for floor planking in an effort to get the bridge into

use. When the commission discovered some auger holes in it, they deducted $25 from the first payment.

Aside from the replacement of occasional siding and the installation of a new roof of sheet metal, White's Bridge today is much the same as it was when erected nearly a century ago. It is built with a type of construction which seems to have enjoyed only a brief popularity, and only in Michigan at that. This was the Brown truss, invented and patented in 1857 by Josiah Brown of Buffalo, New York. This type of bridge resembles the Howe arrangement of "X" panel bracing and counterbracing, but uses lighter and less timber. It contains no upright (or tension) members, and no iron save for bolt connectors at the timber intersections.

Brazee and Walker successfully used this truss for at least four covered bridges in central Michigan, three of which are still in existence. Purchasing timber from a mill at Greenville, where they also built a covered bridge complete with twin sidewalks, the contractors floated select logs down Flat River to a site near Lowell, where they squared and dressed them for use.

Brazee's earliest known covered bridge on the Brown plan was at the lumber town of Falasburg, then a going community of some 200 people on the main stage route from Ionia to Grand Rapids. He built a 100-foot span over the Flat River there in 1862. The routing of the Detroit and Milwaukee Railroad through Lowell, five

224. *Big timber-latticed bridge once straddled Grand River at Ada, Michigan.*

miles to the south, doomed the commercial importance of old Fallasburg. Today only a handful of houses remain, but the covered bridge still serves the area, now known as Fallasburg Park.

In building another covered bridge at Ada, his home base of operations, Jared Brazee took a few liberties with the Brown truss. Instead of costly wrought-iron bolts, he used wooden pins fashioned from hard native oak. Well protected from the elements since 1866, it spans Thornapple River. When a new state highway crossing was built nearby in 1931, the bridge was retained as a historical landmark and pedestrian way.

Brazee's partner, Joseph H. Walker of Grand Rapids, was a Vermonter who had come to Michigan as a baby and who had learned the carpentry trade from his father. His introduction to heavy construction came in building wooden bridges for the Detroit and Milwaukee Railroad. After his association with Brazee he devoted his woodworking talents to the steadier and more lucrative production of fine coffins.

By far the longest existing covered bridge in Michigan today is the Langley Bridge, three miles north of Centerville in St. Joseph County. Stretching 282 feet in three spans across the impounded St. Joseph River, it was framed, floored and roofed in the fall of 1887. Constructed by Pierce Bodner of Parkeville, Langley Bridge is of standard Howe-truss construction. It has fifty-four pieces of $5 \times 12 \times 32$-inch white pine in each of the lower chords, and a like number of 5×9's in the upper stringers. Holding the sturdy braced trusses taut are 180 cast-iron blocks.

The bridge was raised eight feet in 1910 when the Sturgis Power Company's dam and reservoir were built. Concrete caps on the original masonry abutments and piers served for forty years, but scouring action made them suspect. In 1950–51 the St. Joseph County Road Commission restored the bridge, replacing the old foundations, and cantilevering steel beams on them to take some of the weight of traffic.

During an inspection of the job, Superintendent of Roads Paul Pashby inadvertently stepped off into 28 feet of water. The superintendent, according to his own admission, "hadn't been swimming in thirty years." He was fortunate in being able to catch a dangling rope, and was soon hauled to safety.

Still unusually low to the water for any type of river crossing, Langley Bridge is located in a popular recreation area, and is considered one of Southern Michigan's outstanding attractions.

A final existing covered bridge in Michigan occupies a prominent place in Greenfield Village, the extensive collection of historical buildings acquired and arranged by the late Henry Ford.

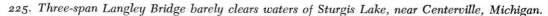

225. Three-span Langley Bridge barely clears waters of Sturgis Lake, near Centerville, Michigan.

226. Ackley Bridge in Henry Ford's Greenfield Village Museum, was brought here from Western Pennsylvania.

Though the automobile magnate once declared that "history is bunk," he certainly aided and abetted the collection and preservation of things historical. Timber by timber, brick by brick, Mr. Ford had the actual landmarks associated with the men he admired taken down and transported to Dearborn for reconstruction in what became a beautiful village directly out of the nineteenth century. Soon the creator of the Model T let it be known that he might add an authentic covered bridge to the spacious grounds.

In a dozen states there are covered bridges pointed out as "the one Henry Ford tried to buy." Some of the claims are true, some spurious. Mr. Ford's agents did look at a number of possible bridges that were slated for removal. Their interest usually had the effect of making each timber of an old landmark suddenly more precious than platinum. Most of the possibilities proved too difficult to consider transporting to Michigan. A side effect of Mr. Ford's seeking an authentic covered bridge was that this outside interest and the magic name of "Ford" heightened local pride. As a result a number of covered spans whose nearby communities had taken them for granted for years and years were retained.

In addition to Thomas Edison, Stephen Foster and the Wright Brothers, Mr. Ford had a particular fondness for William Holmes McGuffey, the schoolmaster from whose "Eclectic Readers" he had learned as a boy. McGuffey was already represented in Greenfield Village by a log schoolhouse brought from the pioneer farm in western Pennsylvania where the educator was born.

Just seven miles south of McGuffey's birthplace in the Keystone State stood a covered bridge

227. Smith Tooker's sidewalked Grand River Bridge, an early landmark of Lansing, Michigan.

228. 1879 drawing of Flint River Bridge on South Street in Flint, Michigan.

over Enslow's Fork of Wheeling Creek. Straddling the line between Greene and Washington counties, it had been erected back in 1832 by Joshua Ackley and Daniel Clouse. When the little 75-foot Pennsylvania span was to be razed after 105 years of service, it was acquired by Ackley's granddaughter, Mrs. Harleigh J. Carroll. She generously *gave* Mr. Ford the bridge.

Because of the connection with his revered Professor McGuffey, the industrialist was of course delighted. In November 1937 Ford's workmen descended on the old Ackley covered bridge and carefully dismantled its oak beams and yellow poplar siding. They stowed it aboard a

229. Bensen Street Bridge over the Titibawassee River at Midland, Michigan.

big Ford truck for the 300-mile trip to Dearborn with all the care of long-distance movers packing heirloom china.

The Ackley Bridge, re-erected at Greenfield Village over an artificial river especially dug to be crossed by it, appears today as though it had always stood there. Few covered bridges have ever found such a pleasant setting for their retirement years, complete with appreciative visitors from all over the world.

Except for the old spans noted at the foregoing locations, the covered bridge in Michigan is a thing of the past. Among the earliest in the state were two over the Grand River at Lansing. A heavy lattice bridge on the Town plan once served Michigan Avenue opposite the state capitol, and stood from 1852 to 1870. It had sidewalks, but may not have been roofed. Another on Franklin Street (now Grand River Avenue) was a neat bridge whose broad roof sheltered a wide roadway and double sidewalks. It was built in 1854 by Smith Tooker, a carpenter-contractor from the Finger Lakes region of New York State. Certain of a building boom when it was decided to establish the state capital at Lansing, Tooker purposely came to Michigan in 1847. His wife was one of the first non-Indian female residents of the newly opened region. Franklin Street Bridge was carried away by flood in 1875, but another Tooker-built span over Cedar River on Cedar Street stood until 1890.

Other Town lattice covered bridges in Michigan were the three-span "Old White" Gratiot Toll

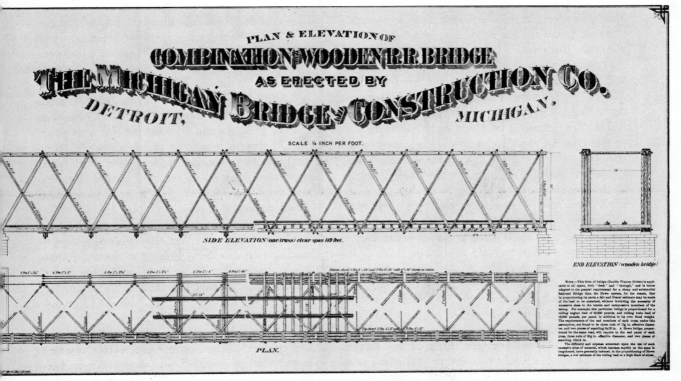

230. *Broadside shows type of construction used by Michigan bridge firm. Truss shown has features of Smith and other patents, but is termed a "double Warren girder"!*

Bridge over Clinton River at Mount Clemens north of Detroit, and the two-span Cook's Bridge over the Thornapple River near Cascade in Kent County.

Over Flint River in Flint were both a covered highway and a housed railroad bridge. Farther north at Midland stood two Howe-truss structures built in 1871 by George F. Keep. The lower of these, spanning the Tittibawassee (pronounced rapidly) River on Benson Street, sported arcaded sidewalks. Both bridges went out in high water during a January storm of 1907.

Near the Indiana line was the well-built crossing of St. Joseph River at Mottville, a two-spanner on the Burr arch plan, dating from 1867. Hahlon Thompson and Joseph Miller erected the bridge in that year, using hand-hewn timbers of whitewood and black walnut, some a substantial sixty feet long.

In the rush to complete a cross-state trunk route in 1921, the Mottville Bridge, still sturdy,

was bypassed by a new concrete highway crossing. The township board, never dreaming that such a bridge might someday become an asset as a tourist attraction, sold the old structure to Roy Berger for $150. After razing the two arched

231. *Purchaser of Mottville, Michigan, bridge realized a good profit from sale of black walnut timbers.*

spans, Berger is reported to have "made a couple of good year's wages" from sale of the huge and valuable timbers.

It was Grand Rapids that could once claim the title of "Michigan's Covered Bridge City." All told, it had six of them within its limits, at three different sites.

The first crossing of the Grand in what was to be the famous furniture-making metropolis was erected in 1844–45. Of seven spans, it was located appropriately enough on Bridge Street, in this case named for Henry P. Bridge, an early settler and sawmill operator from Massachusetts.

The first Bridge Street Bridge was free, financed by a state grant. Soon, with heavy maintenance costs, private enterprise had to be called in to take over the needs of river crossers. The newly formed Grand Rapids Bridge Company in 1852 put $9000 into a second structure on the Bridge Street site, and began a twenty-two-year period of toll-collecting.

1858 was a great year for bridging the Grand River. At Bridge Street the first toll structure was destroyed by fire, and the company rebuilt anew. A few rods to the south another company erected the substantial Pearl Street Bridge, 620 feet long in six spans on the Burr arch-truss plan. A third crossing at Leonard Street was completed in October, bringing the total of the city's covered toll bridges to three. The modest fees of 2 cents per foot passenger appear to have amply paid the proprietors for their investments. A swain of the '60's was considered a big splurger when he spent the 8 cents for a round-trip Sunday afternoon promenade over one of the long, shady bridges high above the breezy waters of the Grand.

A Fourth of July celebration dinner was held in the Pearl Street Bridge after the Civil War ended in 1865. Grand Rapids' returning boys in blue, along with hundreds of townspeople, were served at long wooden tables piled high with turkey, duck, roast chicken and varied desserts. It is hoped that the bridge was well swept and scoured previous to the occasion.

Not long after, Henry Stone decided to demonstrate his new steam-driven threshing machine to admiring city dwellers. Puffing a beautiful trail of black smoke, he clanked down Bridge Street and from his lofty perch overawed the toll-taker, who dubiously allowed the iron-wheeled monster into the dark confines of the bridge.

Belching sparks and steam, the thresher forged ahead under Stone's eager hand, while worried foot passengers scurried for shore. Their misgivings were well founded. Midway of the bridge the machine stalled, and soon embers from her stack had started a brisk blaze in the cobwebby rafters.

"Git out! Git out!" screamed the bridge-tender, as a hastily-formed bucket brigade extinguished the flames.

Henry got rolling again and at length gained

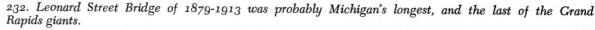
232. *Leonard Street Bridge of 1879-1913 was probably Michigan's longest, and the last of the Grand Rapids giants.*

the west bank of the river, followed by the shouted admonition: ". . . and don't come back over this bridge, ever!"

The trouble was that Henry Stone lived on the East Side, and his new thresher was not exactly amphibious. What to do? Gingerly he made his way down to the Pearl Street Bridge, keeping his fire low and the smoke to a minimum.

Either news of the fire on the bridge above had not reached the toll-taker on Pearl Street, or he considered his bridge fireproof. Henry crossed his palm with silver and was waved grandly on. But, as reported in the Grand Rapids *Herald,* it "just wasn't Stone's day." Well out on the bridge, the creaking floorboards gave way. The cumbersome thresher was left gurgling and smoking, precariously hanging by one huge wheel above the sparkling waters of the Grand River, while her owner chewed his mustache in chagrin.

A greater menace to the Pearl Street Bridge was a seething logjam which came floating downstream with a spring freshet in 1883. Stretched from bank to bank, the sea of cut timber reached clear to the floor of the bridge, and seemed certain to carry it along on its crest, on downriver to Lake Michigan. Crowds fanned out at either end of the well-known landmark to witness its supposed end. Despite the terrific battering of piers and stringers, the bridge held firm.

The City of Grand Rapids bought and freed the three toll bridges in 1873–74. Wrought-iron spans took the place of Bridge Street in 1884 and Pearl Street two years later. At Leonard Street, surprisingly, a new covered bridge was erected in 1879. This bridge, of lattice construction, was built under the direction of William Seckel, Grand Rapids City Engineer, and its ornate portals greeted cross-town travelers until 1913. With eight spans, its 832-foot length is thought to have made it the longest covered bridge ever built in the state of Michigan.

V

ILLINOIS
Crossings of Lincoln

THOUGH comparatively few covered bridges were built in Illinois, those that were have been remarkably long-lived. Over half of those remaining are well over a century old, and date from the days when the state empowered township commissions to build roads and bridges.

Strangely, the name of not one builder of the thirty-odd known existing and former covered bridges in Illinois has been recorded. They were almost without a doubt emigrants from New England and Pennsylvania; local builder-contractors familiar with the details of wooden bridge construction. The dates of their handiwork appear in the old minute books; the men themselves are forgotten.

Oldest in Illinois is the Henderson Creek bridge between Gladstone and Oquawka, a few miles from the Mississippi River and once part of the main-traveled wagon road on the Illinois side. This Burr arch truss was built in 1845–46 and is supposed to be largely composed of black walnut timber. With a highway relocation in 1935, the span was retired and is now a part of a popular roadside park. Picnickers and

233. Roadside park surrounds old Mary's River Bridge, erected to serve private plank road east of Chester, Illinois.

casual visitors still marvel at the sound and gracefully curved arches, and chuckle at the verbose signs on the portals:

FIVE DOLLARS FINE FOR LEADING OR DRIVING
ANY BEAST FASTER THAN A WALK OR DRIVING
MORE THAN THIRTY HEAD OF CATTLE MULES
OR HORSES AT A TIME ON OR ACROSS
THIS BRIDGE

Built during the following decade is a similar covered bridge, also preserved in a state roadside park, and the only remaining structure of its type in southern Illinois. It spans the Little Mary's River east of Chester, and dates from 1854. In that year the Randolph County Plank Road Company laid a one-way wooden highway from Bremen to the river port of Chester, with frequent turnouts for travelers to avoid miring down in the soggy soil. A. E. Hartman, designer-builder of the road, had Little Mary's River bridged as part of the enterprise. Tolls were charged for nearly thirty years, until maintenance proved too much for the proprietor, and both the rotted plank road and its protected bridge were transferred to the county. When a new span was erected by the state in 1930, the old was retained in its little park at the instigation of the Chester Chamber of Commerce.

During his circuit-riding days in Illinois, Abraham Lincoln no doubt occasionally traversed some covered bridges. Four possibilities among those still standing would be Henderson

Creek, Chester, an ancient queenpost truss bridge over Swan Creek in Warren County, and the Thompson Mill Bridge over Kaskaskia River near Cowden. Obviously eligible as having been trod-

234-235. Neat horizontally-sided span over Swan Creek near Greenbush, Illinois.

237. Century-old Hamilton Bridge as it appeared when in use as part of toll crossing of Mississippi River.

236. Henderson Creek Bridge near Gladstone is thought to be the oldest in Illinois, but perhaps was rebuilt.

238. *Former Horse Creek Bridge in Sangamon County, Illinois, a skeleton in the flatlands.*

239. *Wolf Bridge over Spoon River, a rural beauty spot along stream made famous by poet Edgar Lee Masters.*

den on by the Great Emancipator would be the Sangamon County covered bridges in the vicinity of Lincoln's Springfield home. More than likely he crossed their predecessors, but the existing Sugar Creek and Spring Creek bridges near the state capital date from the 1880's. Painted the pleasing red so predominant in Illinois, they are lightly timbered latter-day adaptions of the well-known Burr arch-truss plan.

In the river town of Hamilton is one of America's most unusual covered bridges, and one

with a checkered history. It was built in 1869 as a portion of a toll structure erected across the Mississippi River by the Keokuk and Hamilton Bridge Company. Since the lengthy interstate connection was to serve both a rail line and a wagon road, its Howe trusses were built high and heavy. After a dozen years of service the main bridge was wrecked when struck on November 4, 1881 by the excursion boat *War Eagle*.

In the subsequent rebuilding, this 169-foot portion was moved to a river backwater on the

240-241. *Sangamon County, Illinois, still has covered bridges over Sugar and Spring creeks on roads which Abraham Lincoln travelled, but they were erected after his lifetime.*

Illinois side, where for many years it served as part of a long causeway leading to the main bridge. Some of its unusual features include the tie rods and turnbuckles underneath the flooring, used in truing up the span in the same manner applied to old-time railroad boxcars. Despite the ample 12-foot-10-inch overhead clearance, a unique hinged antismash bar was installed on the portal, preventing both passage and damage by extra-high loads. Now retired, the massive red-painted bridge is still a prominent Hamilton landmark.

Three other covered bridges stand in northwestern Illinois. On a gravel road between Douglas and Gilson is Wolf Bridge, spanning the Spoon River made famous by poet Edgar Lee Masters' well-read anthology. Also red, with white trim on the board-and-batten finish, this bridge has the protection against fire provided by interior whitewash, and is reached on either side by old iron approach spans. In a beautiful country setting, it is one of the delightful surprises of the Illinois landscape.

Near Princeton is another well-kept old Red Bridge, this one over Big Bureau Creek. A committee called "The Union Bridge Company" was responsible for its existence, using funds furnished by Bureau County and Dover Township, which were matched by private subscription. 1863 saw the bridge a reality, and the centenarian is still sturdy and well traveled. On its portals is another of the old wordy traffic warnings. This one reads:

> FIVE DOLLARS FINE FOR DRIVING MORE THAN TWELVE HORSES MULES OR CATTLE AT ANY ONE TIME OR FOR LEADING ANY BEAST FASTER THAN A WALK ON OR ACROSS THIS BRIDGE.

Even a slow-plodding traveler had to pause a bit to digest all that before venturing across, and "any beast" is interpreted by some to include the shiny products of Detroit. A local Princeton merchant's advertising sign inside is more to the point:

> HAYWARD SELLS GROCERIES CHEAP.

Perhaps the acme of covered bridge adver-

242. Red Bridge near Princeton retains one of the wordy signs which typified 19th century Illinois spans.

tising has been achieved by a religious group who placarded the Swan Creek Bridge southeast of Greenbush, Illinois. During the winter of 1963 their sign was bold and prominent on the little span:

> LET US FACE IT. YOU TURN OR YOU BURN.
> JESUS SAVES.

Beyond, the road became an impassable mudhole.

243. Bear Creek Bridge south of Lima, Illinois. Second admonition on portal went unheeded and bridge was burned in 1933.

244. *Unpaved streets of Rockford, Illinois, led to a covered bridge in 1855.*

VI
MISSOURI
Show Me Some Bridges

TRANSPORTATION in Missouri followed the rivers, and then took up with the iron horse. Fords and ferries served for crossing streams during the state's early years, and the covered bridge was late in coming to "show-me" country.

The first recorded timbered "tunnel bridge" in Missouri is said to have been built in 1851, when Perche Creek west of Columbia was spanned to provide a more permanent crossing for the Boon's Lick Trail. Travis Burroughs, the contractor, built the span predominately of oak timber and received $2500 for the job.

Though the names are similar, Missouri's Meremec River (Indian: Catfish) has no relation to New Hampshire's Merrimack (Indian: Swift Water) back East, though both were spanned by covered bridges. The St. Louis suburb of Fenton was the site of such a structure as early as 1854, and farther upstream a long-forgotten covered bridge served Smizer's Mill and Whiskey Distillery, connecting with the Pacific Railroad's Meremec Station on the north bank.

Other bridges were built for the roads which converge on St. Louis, at places like Union and DeSoto. Robert Elliott, an Illinois builder, brought the Burr arch truss to Paris in Monroe County, spanning the Middle Fork of Salt River in 1857.

Strong feelings between North and South kept Missouri in a constant unsettled condition for more than a decade. As a border state battleground, with both Union and Confederate troops ranging the hills and valleys, it was not a wise thing to construct anything new in the way of bridges until hostilities were ended.

With the late start, the delays of wartime, and then the approach of the age of iron, Missouri had but few covered bridges. The majority of the less than thirty of which there is record date from the Reconstruction days that followed the Civil War, down to 1886. For the most part they dotted northern Missouri, and only one is known to have stood in the Ozark region to the south.

The Chicago firm of Stone & Boomer erected patented Howe-truss railroad bridges all over the state, with much of the timber coming from Osage County in central Missouri (see Chapter X). It was only natural for postwar contractors and builders to erect their highway spans on the same well-proven plan.

Good main timbers of white oak and poplar were available, and black walnut planking was more than adequate weatherboarding. Before the days of tin roofs the shingling was usually white pine. As for paint, red was and still is the favorite color.

Builders like Joseph Lansman of Cape Girardeau County, Joseph Elliott of Monroe and Charles McQuoid up in Knox County used the perfected Howe plans and never had to worry about piece sizes and proportions as in prewar days when bridges were constructed solely "by judgment."

At Burfordville, Lansman started a bridge over Whitewater Creek in 1860, and came back after the war to complete it. With its 140-foot clear span, it is by far the largest covered bridge in Missouri. Located above a dam and beside the old Bollinger Flour Mill, its site is among the most scenic and photogenic of any covered span in the nation.

Nearby over Whitewater was the former Allenville covered bridge, tightly trimmed with board-and-batten finish. Mr. Ruff, its builder, is reported to have been so strict that he would fire

245. By-passed now, this bridge spans the old channel of Locust Creek west of Laclede, Missouri.

any carpenter who drove a nail so carelessly as to leave the rounded imprint of his hammer on the wood.

246. Nearest to St. Louis is Sandy Creek Bridge on the old Le May Ferry Road near Goldman, Missouri.

Five covered bridges in addition to Burford-ville still span Missouri streams. No longer in use, but preserved, are the bridge over Locust Creek west of Laclede, and Noah's Ark Bridge in Platte County to the north of Kansas City. This last received its name from Noah Berry, who served as county judge at the time the bridge was erected in 1878.

Paris had bad luck with its oldest, Elliott-built covered bridge, situated just three blocks from the heart of town and dating from 1857. The arch truss was strengthened and completely renovated in 1953, only to be undermined and lost to Salt River floodwaters three years later. Another example of the skill of Elliott and his bridge-building family still spans the Elk Fork to the south of Paris.

Nearest to St. Louis is the Sandy Creek Bridge on the old Lemay Ferry Road near Goldman in Jefferson County. Originally built as part of a county road-construction program in 1872, the crossing was included with a contract done by John H. Morse. Since Mr. Morse came from the same town (Sutton, Massachusetts) as the bridge-building Boomer brothers (see Chapter

X), it was only natural that he selected their favorite Howe plan of construction. Even when a freshet wrenched and wrecked the all-white-pine span, contractor Henry Steffin used half the old timbers to rebuild it in kind in 1886. Today it still serves local traffic, only twenty miles south of the St. Louis metropolitan area.

One Missouri bridge was built as late as 1903, serving the tiny community of Prairie Lick between Boonville and Pilot Grove. New as covered bridges go, this one was hardly a dozen years old when it became a place of mystery and acquired a bona fide ghost.

During the spring of 1917, everybody for miles around Prairie Lick began to be aware that the bridge was haunted. In the dark hours after midnight weird sounds issued from its gloomy interior, and a horse would balk at passage. Farmers began to take long detours to avoid this crossing of the Petit Saline, or simply never venture out after dark. It was bad enough that the structure creaked and swayed in the wind, but to have it inhabited by spooks was too much.

Things reached a climax one night at a carnival in Boonville. Tales of the haunted bridge were getting out of hand in the retelling, and an adventurous young man named Walter Brown determined to put an end to them. Partly seriously and partly in jest he told a group of hangers-on he'd investigate that very night, provided they went with him.

They agreed, and fortified by several stiff ones under his belt, Brown borrowed a rifle and set out for the bridge in his Model T. Behind him trundled some 15 cars, giving the witch hunt the status of an invading army. The procession wound out along the dirt road between thickly wooded hills, and down to the river bottom and the bridge.

A signal from the intrepid leader brought the parade to a halt. Engines sputtered and died. Lights were doused. In the silence, the only sounds were of cricket, peepfrog and owl, punctuated by an occasional hiccough.

Walter Brown's Ford was braked at the foot of the bridge approach. He vaulted out and reached back to light a gas lantern. With the minutes ticking by on his pocket Ingersoll he sat on the running board and read the time: 12:15 A.M.

Just then a loud clanking rattle issued from the dark bridge, followed by unearthly scraping thumps, bumps and inhuman sounds. It was enough to raise hair on a bald man, and some of the less fortified occupants of the darkened cars were ready to hightail it for Boonville.

Brown raised his lantern and two bright eyes peered unswervingly at him from the cobwebbed rafters. Silently raising his rifle, the young man took aim.

Blam!

The well-directed shot between the eyes reverberated through the hollow confines of the bridge like a string of land mines. Clutching his lantern, Brown rushed forward, and found that an enormous raccoon had plummeted to the floor. Around the animal's neck was a leather strap to which was attached a length of heavy trace chain. In his nocturnal foraging from a hideaway in the bridge's "attic," the escaped pet had been dragging the chain and scaring the wits out of both equine and human travelers. The spook hunter picked up the twenty-seven-pound carcass and emerged triumphant. One by one the car lights of the "posse" came on to illuminate the scene.

"Here's your ghost!" he called, rattling the chain.

247. "Noah's Ark" Bridge in original site over Little Platte River. Span has been moved to Tracy, Missouri, fairgrounds.

SPRING HILL FARM.—The residence of Capt. George Smizer is pleasantly situated upon the south bank of the Merrimac River and adjoining Merrimac Station on the Pacific Railroad, twenty miles from St. Louis.   The dwelling house, beautifully located upon an eminence overlooking the farm, gives a fine view of nearly three miles of the Railroad.— Four hundred acres of fine alluvial soil is under a high state of cultivation in the valley as seen in the foreground, while ample pasturage for cattle is found in the fine blue grass pastures in the back ground.   Five running Springs of pure limestone water are found upon the farm.   The mills are capable of manufacturing fifty barrels of Flour, twenty-five barrels of Whiskey, and five thousand feet of Lumber per day, whilst two thousand hogs may be fed with the greatest ease at the distilery.

57

248. Old engraving delineates Smizer's Mill and Whiskey Distillery at Meremec Station, Missouri.

Other men have fought and won pitched battles in covered bridges and never received the acclaim which came to Walter Brown. For his prowess in bringing the haunt to bay, he was hailed for years as "The Hero of Prairie Lick Bridge."

VII

IOWA
Flat-tops in the Cornfields

FOR many years it was not realized that Iowa was part of the national covered-bridge picture, and that there were still a good dozen such spans to be found among the stalks out where the tall corn grows.

Hotbed of covered bridges is Madison County, a farmbelt quadrangle to the southwest of Des Moines. Winterset, the county seat, has been called the "Covered Bridge Capital of the Middle West," and has certainly been busy taking steps to validate its claim.

Madison still has seven covered bridges within its borders. A number of counties in Vermont, Pennsylvania, Ohio, Indiana and Oregon have considerably more than that number, but only a few—notably Parke County in Indiana—consider their old timbered tunnels as honest-to-goodness assets to the county.

The friendly people of Winterset and the Madison County farmland are to be heartily congratulated for the example they have set in making their covered bridges attractive, accessible and a mecca for thousands of tourists every year.

Time was when Madison had about fourteen covered bridges, built during the two decades after 1870. All were constructed on the Town lattice plan so popular in New England, built in this area of Iowa long after the type was considered obsolete elsewhere.

H. P. Jones seems to have been the most prolific covered-bridge builder in the Winterset region, and he added new wrinkles to the time-tested Town "mode" of erection. For substructure he used caisson piers, and he buttressed the sides of his spans with taut guy rods attached to protruding floor beams. Inside, his single-web lattices were usually given the extra reinforcement of auxiliary arches, queenposts, or a combination

of the two. Jones' most startling innovation was the virtual elimination of the conventional high-pitched roof. His bridges are tightly weather-boarded to the eaves, and their roofs have only a very slight pitch. One writer, perhaps thinking these structures were built or altered to save the work and expense of raftering, has called them "Madison's marvelous makeshifts." This is untrue. Close examination shows them to have been carefully planned and extremely well built. These squared tubular covered bridges in Iowa have a unique appearance duplicated only in a few other places in the world.

Reduced in numbers by flood, ice jam, modernization, vandalism and just plain indifference, by 1948 the count of Madison County covered

249. *Rural view "near Villisca, Iowa," in 1882.*

250. *Cedar Bridge over Cedar Creek northeast of Winterset, Madison County.*

ing of a red covered bridge, offering information. The local post of the American Legion has done a fine job of placing signs at strategic intersections, pointing the way to the bridges, and anyone supplied with the Chamber of Commerce map will find it difficult to go astray.

Five of the bridges are of the rare flat-topped variety, while the two oldest have the more familiar pitched roof. A ninety-mile tour, centering on Winterset, will take the covered-bridge hunter to all of them in a day, though a more leisurely two-day junket is recommended.

Each bridge, though similar in construction,

251. *Madison County's flat-topped Hogback Bridge over North River northwest of Winterset.*

252. *Flat-topped Roseman Bridge over Middle River west of Pammel State Park, Madison County.*

bridges was down to seven. In that year a movement was started to save the remaining spans and make them one of the prime attractions of the area. The Madison County Historical Society and various civic-minded individuals sparked the drive. Their enthusiasm soon spread to the County Board of Supervisors, which appropriated funds for the restoration and continued upkeep of the bridges. Foundations were strengthened, approach rails replaced, trusses tightened and tuned up. The old names for the bridges were revived, and each span given a simple board on which they were stenciled, together with the date of erection. Best of all, liberal coats of bright red paint were applied to every one of the seven survivors, and the already colorful landscape enriched.

The campaign to publicize the bridges has far exceeded the original modest expectations. From spring until late fall the excellent explanatory route folders distributed by the Winterset Chamber of Commerce are in great demand, and it is estimated that some eight to ten thousand people make a full or partial tour of the county's unique bridges each year. One of the first things that greets the Winterset visitor is a huge wall paint-

has its own peculiar beauty of setting, and good
gravel roads lead through some unforgettable
panoramas of field, wood and stream. Especially
scenic are the two bridges to the west of U.S.
169, Hogback, reached by way of a high ridge,
and McBride, with its red and white paint a
colorful contrast to blue sky and black loam soil.

One of the nearest to Winterset is Holliwell
Bridge over Middle River, where Town lattice,
arch and queenpost are all combined to make an
extra-sturdy truss. Something different in the
way of warning signs is here, too:

$50 FINE FOR CROSSING THIS BRIDGE FASTER
THAN A WALK, OR ANY CUTTING, DISFIGURING
OR DRAGGING LOGS ACROSS.

Elsewhere in Iowa are four more covered
bridges, all equally scenic in setting, but not as
well publicized. Just southeast of Des Moines is
the old Owens Bridge moved from near Carlisle.
Though abandoned and almost forgotten when
the highway and channel of North River were
changed in the '30's, in recent years it was
found to be still in place and in remarkably good
shape. Thanks to local interest, the old white-
painted Howe-truss span was pulled from the
tangle of underbrush which had all but obscured
its continued existence and re-erected in a new
county park.

In Marion County stand two more back-
country survivors of the wooden-bridge contractor's art. Hammond Bridge, at the Armour
Versteg Farm south of Attica, is a well-kept old
red Howe truss. West of Marysville a dead-end
road leads to a little-used crossing perched on
slim pilings over South Cedar Creek. It is slated
for re-erection in Knoxville.

The remote Marysville span is of lattice, but
differs from the regular type in that the trusses
are only three-quarters as deep. Originally built
some fifteen miles away, it was moved here in
1926. The contractor, laying out his full webs of
lattices in an adjacent field, carefully indicated
the ultimate destination of each piece of timber.
Still plain are the black-painted letters and
Roman numerals, with E and W for East and
West sides, and TC, MC and BC for top, middle
and bottom chords.

Iowa's oldest and easternmost covered bridge

253. *Imes Bridge, oldest of Madison County, Iowa's,
well-kept crossings has served on two sites.*

254. *Hammond Bridge serves prosperous Iowa farm
country south of Attica.*

255. *Little Marysville Bridge has stood at two locations and will soon serve a third in Knoxville, Iowa.*

256. *English Creek span east of Durham, Iowa, was recent victim of that continual enemy of covered bridges, fire.*

257. *Caisson piers uphold Skunk River Bridge south of Delta, Iowa.*

was built in 1869 south of Delta in Keokuk County. On the Burr plan, it straddles the North Fork of Skunk River on caissons and a new concrete pier. Despite its decrepit appearance, like the flat-roofed wooden wonders of Winterset, it has stood a full century, an age which the builders of covered bridges seldom dreamed their handiwork would reach.

VIII

WISCONSIN

Lone Survivor

THERE are records of only a few covered bridges being built in Wisconsin. Again, it was a case of erecting "make-do" bridges during settlement and early pioneering days. By the time that permanent villages had sprung up, and roads built to connect them, there was enough prosperity to replace fords and bridges of piling with wrought-iron and steel spans.

At the western edge of the state, one of the earliest covered bridges spanned the Wisconsin River near its mouth at Bridgeport, six miles east of Prairie du Chien. First erected in 1857 and rebuilt in 1892, the crossing was a long, tightly enclosed two-span Howe truss. It was close to the water, with a draw for river naviga-

tion on the Bridgeport side, plus lengthy trestling stretching to the south shore.

Bridgeport was always operated as a privately owned toll bridge. The opportunist who did the best with it was Milwaukee-born Harry Lathrop, who came to town as station agent for the Milwaukee Railroad. Lathrop presided over the red railroad buildings perched precariously along the river bank. Early in his years at Bridgeport, the toll bridge was threatened by high waters. As the Wisconsin lapped at the wide floor boards, the owner wrung his hands and publicly wished he had chosen some other business. Harry Lathrop "on a dumb hunch" bought the bridge right then and there for $6000. It looked as though Harry might just as readily have thrown

258. *Boscobel, Wisconsin, became a city in order to meet the expense of building this bridge in 1874.*

259. Now by-passed and strengthened with a new center pier, Cedarburg Bridge is Wisconsin's only old-time covered bridge.

his money in the raging river, but by the next dawn the flood crest had passed, and the station agent was in possession of a going toll bridge.

With the advent of automobile traffic, and the routing of a trunk cross-state highway over the bridge, Lathrop's investment became known as "Harry's Gold Mine." In addition to thousands of cars, a great number of cattle, hogs and sheep were brought over the bridge to be shipped to market on the railroad. Toll-bridge owner Lathrop got 3 cents a head for swine, sheep and

260. Town lattice trusses support surviving Wisconsin covered bridge north of Cedarburg.

"neat critturs," while Milwaukee Railroad agent Lathrop added his commission for shipment.

Rates also specified: 10 cents for a horseback rider, led horse or bicycle, 5 cents for a foot passenger, 20 cents a team, a quarter per automobile and half a dollar for a truck.

It wasn't all gravy, of course. When the trestle approach on the south side was carried away in an ice jam, the genial proprietor had considerable out-of-pocket expense to replace it in 1920.

In addition to being an astute businessman, Harry Lathrop was a flute player, beekeeper, traveler and poet. He was quite content to face the inevitable in 1931, and accepted $15,151.00 from the State of Wisconsin to scrap his by then ramshackle old bridge in favor of a free high-level crossing.

At Boscobel, about twenty miles upstream from Bridgeport, the Wisconsin River was also crossed by a toll bridge. In order to take on the bonded indebtedness necessary to span the navigable river, Boscobel sought and received a city charter. Only then did the bridge project get the go-ahead.

Erected in 1874 under the direction of a Mr. Pertell of Milwaukee, this was an odd 655-foot combination of iron from Pittsburgh and wood from Green Bay. From the north bank, or Manhattan side, a single covered span connected with a pivoted 150-foot draw built of iron. Next came two more covered Howe truss spans, and then a fixed-iron truss carried on to the Boscobel side.

Wisconsin historian Reuben Goldthwaites, who admittedly had an aversion to covered bridges, described the Boscobel fabrication as "an ugly, clumsy structure, housed in like a tunnel and dark as a pocket."

Though not as well traveled or as lucrative a proposition as Bridgeport, the Boscobel Toll Bridge kept going for sixty years. The city at last sold out to the state in 1935 for $22,778.00. A new, free crossing replaced the hybrid spans in 1937.

Another covered bridge in southern Wisconsin seems to have achieved more fame since its passing than while it was still in existence. This was the Clarence Bridge, spanning Sugar River three miles southwest of Brodhead, which stood from 1864 to 1934.

261. *Cedar Creek Bridge north of Cedarburg, Wisconsin, in its original rural setting.*

In Brodhead, Frank H. Engebretson had for years made a living at painting his neighbors' barns. Engebretson didn't just paint his barns one flat color; he embellished them with over a hundred huge murals of scenic landscapes, done in bright oils. After the Clarence Bridge was torn down, this self-taught "barnyard muralist" immortalized the span's scenic setting on a small barn in Brodhead. Featured in news syndicate releases, and in *Life,* Mr. Engebretson's barn art and the old Clarence covered bridge received national attention.

Other Wisconsin covered bridges once stood over the Neshonic River at West Salem, and over the Sheboygan River on Lower Falls Road between the busy cities of Sheboygan and Kohler. What was perhaps the most northern covered wooden bridge in the state was a 3-spanner of 1869–80 which spanned the Chippewa River at Chippewa Falls. Along the Baraboo River at Rock Springs and Butterfield's in Sauk County were a pair of lattice-covered spans erected by a local builder named Dodd.

The bridge-building worth of the white pine from the Baraboo Ranges was appreciated as far distant as Ozaukee County, north of Milwaukee. When a bridge near Cedarburg was projected in 1876, all the timber and planking for a Town lattice structure were cut and squared at a mill near Baraboo, and then hauled some seventy-five miles to the bridge site. The single 120-foot span, erected over Cedar Creek on a town road, turned out to be a credit to its unknown builder. In addition to regular siding, he gave his work an attractive board-and-batten finish and a good coat of red paint.

Through the years the suburbs of Milwaukee stretched northward, and what was once a rural road past Cedarburg to the covered bridge is now a heavily traveled commuter's highway. A center pier was placed beneath the truss in 1927, and as early as 1940 the bridge was tabbed for permanent preservation and maintenance as a historic monument by the Ozaukee County Highway Commission. After years of discussion, during which the bridge continued to bear greater and greater traffic burdens, it was at last decided to bypass the span. This was accomplished in 1962.

Now weathered to a silver gray and retired at last, Wisconsin's only authentic old-time covered bridge can be found just north of the five-corner intersection of Routes 60 and 143 out of Cedarburg. A well-known local landmark of considerable importance, it is well deserving of its preservation and commemoration.

IX

All Gone Now

Though the records are slim, it seems probable that at one time or another there were authentic covered bridges, either for highways or railways, in forty-two of the fifty states.

On the Middle Western plains, a trio of covered spans served rail lines in Nebraska, but no covered highway bridges are known to have been in existence in that state. The same is true for Oklahoma and the Dakotas. Development of highway systems in those states came late and coincided with the spreading use of iron and steel.

Two states of the Middle West, however, can contribute to the lore and legend of covered bridges, even though their ghostly river crossings are no more.

KANSAS--Relic on Big Stranger

262. *Former John Bell Bridge over Big Stranger Creek northeast of Jarbalo, Kansas.*

FORT LEAVENWORTH, ON ITS high bluff above the wide Missouri River, was a staging point for thousands of homesteaders in the days just prior to the Civil War. From there they left on their west-bound treks, singly or in groups, depending on the distances to be covered in their journeys, threading over the rolling country which soon flattened into the seemingly interminable plains of Kansas.

About ten miles out of Leavenworth, the old trails brought the pioneers to the fording of Big Stranger Creek, a good place to make camp for the first night. The stream got its name from the Indian "O-keet-sha," which in addition to meaning "stranger" signifies "an aimless wandering," certainly well descriptive of this meandering watercourse.

Three crossings of Big Stranger were popular: the Fort Riley Road at Easton, the Lecompton Road east of Springdale, and the Perryville Road northeast of Jarbalo. These sites, plus another at Farmington, became the locations of the only covered bridges known to have been erected in Kansas.

One well-circulated story attributes the construction of the four covered spans over Big Stranger to Colonel Albert Sidney Johnston (1803–62), later to become the fiery Confederate general who died in the Battle of Shiloh (or Pittsburg Landing). While in command of Fort Leavenworth, Johnston doubtless had wishes to speed western immigration on its way, which naturally called for more permanent crossings of Big Stranger Creek than the existing fords.

More accurate are the military records, which show that the Colonel left Fort Leavenworth for Utah in 1856, and never returned to the post. He may possibly have ordered the erection of the Easton Bridge, built during Johnston's last year in Kansas, and this gave rise to the story of his responsibility for all of the trail crossings.

The prosaic truth was that the Leavenworth county commissioners laid out roads along the old wagon trails, and let contracts for the building of bridges in the usual orderly manner. This was done for the crossing at Springdale in 1858.

County records show that George Dickinson, appointed to superintend construction of "the bridge at Russell's Mill on the Lecompton Road," finished the job himself after a contractor named Barr defaulted.

Dickinson's Springdale Bridge, completed in 1859, was of Howe-truss construction, a regulation patent design of twelve panels. Since the creek had a nasty habit of getting out of its confines each spring, Dickinson founded his single 130-foot span on solid granite piers set away from the banks, reaching it by short approach spans on either side.

Of similar construction, the John Bell Bridge on the Perryville Road to Jarbalo went up in 1866, and the span at Farmington at about the same time.

All four covered bridges stood for seventy-odd years, a good indication of worthy design and fine workmanship. Replacement came with the expansion of the Kansas state highway system. When the others were torn down, a relocation of Kansas Route 92 bypassed the Springdale Bridge in 1932, and the old span, its boards flapping and red paint fading, served only as a little-used

263. Springdale Bridge west of Leavenworth was completely restored by the State of Kansas, only to be destroyed by fire in 1958.

short cut south to the bottomland along the creek.

As the last and only covered bridge in Kansas, the semiabandoned bridge received a fair share of attention from historians. Late in 1945 the Kansas State Highway Commission was induced to take over the span for preservation.

The Commission's workers did a leisurely but excellent job of restoration, with complete residing and roofing. The old Howe trusses were trued up and strengthened where necessary. As a restful, scenic picnic spot, guarded by the sheltering branches of a huge old sycamore, the renovated structure had every expectation of standing for another century. For eleven years it was again used by light traffic and admired by hundreds of tourists.

In September 1958 the good work of preserving the hundred-year-old landmark came to nothing. A nearby farmer reported hearing a loud clap of thunder during an early-morning electrical storm, and saw flames when he got up at 5 A.M. Twenty minutes later the old span lay hissing and smoldering in the waters of Big Stranger, and Kansas had lost its last covered bridge.

MINNESOTA--*Gone to the Fair*

THOUGH TIMBER-RICH, and populated with people with bridge-building traditions and know-how, there is record of only three covered bridges in the entire state of Minnesota. What bridges were originally built to cross the many streams appear to have been crude and temporary open wooden affairs, without the permanence of protection from northern rains and snows. When these simple, uncovered bridges had served their purpose, the age of iron spans was in full sweep.

On the Red River Trail, between St. Cloud and St. Joseph in Stearns County, the Sauk River was spanned by a covered bridge at Waite's Crossing. Built in 1870 and replaced in 1902, it was prob-

ably the farthest north of any covered bridge in the Midwest.

At Hastings stood another of the state's covered bridges. This one spanned the Vermillion River above a flour mill and waterfall. In the 1890's a spring freshet carried off the span. For a full twenty minutes it teetered and swayed on the brink of the falls, caught amid ice cakes on a projecting cooper shop. As local sports were about to take bets, the bridge wrenched loose before the onslaught of wild water, and was dashed to pieces in the gorge below.

Minnesota's last surviving covered bridge once served the village of Zumbrota in Goodhue County. At the crossing of the North Branch of

264. *Minnesota's Zumbrota covered bridge, long a fairground concession stand, now awaits restoration over the river it originally spanned.*

the Zumbro River on the highway between Rochester and St. Paul, Zumbrota was first settled in 1856 by a company of immigrants under Samuel Shaffee of the Strafford Western Immigration Company.

Two successive bridges of unseasoned timber served the raw village's main street until 1869, when the company raised $5800 for the erection of a more substantial piece of work. The new structure was the job of a local carpenter, Evander L. Kingsbury. The plan was that of the Town lattice, popular still in New England but by that time only spottily used elsewhere. Mr. Kingsbury utilized native white-pine timbers, hauled inland from a mill on the Mississippi River at Red Wing. The planks were pinned together with turned white-oak dowels. Though these wooden tree nails were treated with linseed oil and red iron oxide, the bridge itself had no preservatives and was not originally housed in.

Fortunately Zumbrota's village fathers soon voted money to roof and weatherboard the new bridge, and it was given a trim board-and-batten finish on both portals and sides. The man who did the covering estimated his quantities so well that he was able to cart home all the scrap lumber left from the job in a single wheelbarrow.

The bridge was kept neat with successive coats of red, and later white paint. Over the years one of the duties of the village marshal was to nightly illuminate the bridge by means of a kerosene lantern hung in the center, and raised and lowered by a rope. Youthful Zumbrotans thought it great fun to tie knots in the lantern cord, and substitute water for the marshal's kerosene.

Maintained as a village bridge for over fifty years, the Zumbro River span on Main Street continued as part of the state highway system for another decade. When replacement time came in 1932, it was decided to preserve the bridge in the Goodhue County Fairgrounds. William Henke took the contract to move the old lattice structure for $600, and spent 189 actual hauling hours to transport it to its new site.

Flat on the fairground, the bridge was first put to use in housing the poultry exhibit, and was given a new metal roof. Later, with a counter cut along its side, it became an oasis for thirsty fair-goers as the beer concession stand. In this altered state and joyful atmosphere, the hulk of Minnesota's sole example of the covered bridge builder's art survives today.

It may not always be thus. In recent years a local group, the Zumbrota Covered Bridge Society, has been formed for the express purpose of again moving the old bridge superstructure to a more dignified final resting place, this time to a new site over the Zumbro River which it spanned so long.

X

Wood to Weld an Iron Empire
Covered Railroad Bridges

ALL but forgotten today are the gaunt, smoke-stained covered wooden bridges which once served America's vast network of iron rails. Railroads have been the nation's greatest bridge builders; if all the bridges used on the railways of the United States were placed end to end, they would cover a distance of about 3750 miles. A conservative estimate is that half this distance was originally built using wood, and that there were at least 1000 miles of covered bridges exclusively serving the railway system at one time or another. Most company payrolls had to include a bygone occupation, that of "bridge watcher." This was a man or men assigned to bridge sites to inspect the structure after the passing of each train. Firemen were sternly instructed to close their ashpans, and engineers to shut off steam when crossing wooden bridges, which must have been a nuisance.

Where were all these covered railroad bridges? Just about everywhere. Railroads had to have cheap, direct river crossings. If a surveyor plotted the cross-country route of a new line, he indicated bridges where any sizable stream mean-

265. Howe's patent truss for railroad bridges was still being advertised in Ohio as late as 1885.

dered across the proposed path of the iron horse. There was no quibbling about a better angle of approach or more easily prepared abutment sites half a mile downstream; when the rails reached a watercourse it was bridged then and there.

Stone was often difficult to obtain, and structural iron not yet available or trusted. Wood could be cheaply bought near the spots where it was to be used, and could be speedily transformed into usable building timbers.

Hundreds of miles of railroads were built in the Middle West before 1840. Of necessity the engineers of the various lines had to rely on the types of bridges already in use along parallel wagon roads. Deep, wide and fast-flowing streams had to have spans with few intermediate piers. For these the first railroad bridge designers specified some kind of wooden arch, surmounted by a platform deck.

Ithiel Town's 1820 lattice plan was a New England favorite for highway bridges. To make his truss stronger and capable of carrying heavier moving loads, the canny Connecticut inventor doubled the lattice web of planking and made the depth of the trusses greater to accommodate the smokestack and cab of a high-wheeled locomotive.

Some Middle Western railroad-bridge contractors preferred Colonel S. H. Long's patented frame-truss bridge of 1830, and the type had its supporters in a number of regions. Ithiel Town promoted his bridge for railroad use while seeking and carrying out architectural assignments around the country. Stephen Long, almost continuously in service with the Army's topographical engineers, had little time to push his bridge patent, but fortunately was on loan a number of times to plan the routes of infant railroad

HOWE'S PATENT TRUSS

T. H. HAMILTON,
Bridge Builder and General Contractor, - - Toledo, C

OHIO PENITENTIARY, AT COLUMBUS, OHIO.

266. Scioto River Railroad Bridge at Columbus, Ohio, is featured in 1857 illustration.

companies. Often he was in a position to suggest the use of his invention in the subsequent building.

Both Town and Long were represented by agents for the sale of their patent bridge plans and rights. They also exchanged notes in the public press (usually polite) concerning the relative merits of their rival bridge plans. Since both designs were basically good, the railroad companies came to specify "either Town or Long" spans in their building proposals, and were prepared to accept whichever type a successful bidder chose to erect.

Historian Charles Francis Adams once remarked that "the simplest of railroad bridges is an inexplicable mystery to at least ninety-nine persons out of a hundred." One of the hundredth persons was a Massachusetts house builder and millwright whose entry into the field brought about a near monopoly in railroad bridge-building. He was William Howe, whose truss patents of 1840 marked the end of bridges being built entirely of wood, and the beginning of the use of iron components. Primarily a bridge for railroads, the Howe truss could be quickly and cheaply built of the greenest wood. Its secret of success lay in the introduction of iron tension rods to the truss. These could be adjusted and re-adjusted long after the bridge was in service, with trains rolling over it to make money for the railroad's promoters.

It took a few years for the Howe truss to become known and accepted. But once established, proposal after proposal called for "a substantial Howe bridge, well weatherboarded and roofed." Railway engineers who clung to the specification of Town or Long all-wooden types were considered ultraconservative. As the darling of the railroads, the ubiquitous Howe truss enjoyed a thirty-year reign of supremacy.

This unusual acceptance was not accomplished without a great deal of planning and energetic promotion, particularly on the part of a group of determined New Englanders who lauded the virtues of the Howe patent at every opportunity. It was not a coincidence that they also happened to control the sales rights to the new bridge.

William Howe himself was content to be just the inventor, a friendly man who liked music and the good things in life which his bridge royalty

267. *Amasa Stone, Jr.*

payments brought him.

More of a go-getter was Howe's wife's brother, Amasa Stone, Jr. A young cabinetmaker breaking into heavy contracting, Stone foresaw the potential in rights to a bridge which every line of the fast-expanding American railway network would surely need. Teaming with Azuriah Boody, a Canadian-born ex-schoolteacher and railroad brakeman, Amasa Stone scrounged up $40,000 to buy exclusive rights for building the Howe bridge in New England. The two formed a company to build bridges, employed their relatives and friends to learn the work, and laid the foundation for a dynasty of bridge-building firms that would blanket the nation.

After a few years' apprenticeship with Boody, Stone & Co., three other Stone brothers and nearly a dozen other men related by marriage went on to form their own bridge-contracting firms. For the most part young men in their twenties, they took advantage of the bridge-building bonanza which was sweeping westward.

In 1849 Amasa Stone, Jr. moved to Cleveland, Ohio. There, with two new partners, he took on the complete contracting of the Cleveland, Columbus and Cincinnati Railroad. The line was a showplace for the patent wooden Howe trusses, mostly of the deck variety and grandly erected on high stone masonry.

Azuriah Boody also found new rivers to cross in Ohio, and further good fortune. Operating out of Toledo, he pushed the Wabash Railroad on across Indiana, and for years was one of its principal directors.

With the original proprietors of the Howe patents elevated to railroad magnates, the rights were sublet to others. Thatcher, Burt & McNary

took over the work in Ohio. A. L. Maxwell, based in Knoxville, Tennessee, was responsible for bridges in Dixie.

The youngest Stone brother was Andros, who contracted for Howe-truss bridges farther west. Aged twenty-seven, he arrived in Chicago in 1851, armed with exclusive rights for the nation's best railroad bridge. With him came a partner, his wife's brother Lucius B. Boomer, another Massachusetts man to whom the magic word "west" was synonymous with opportunity. Despite the fact that both Stone and Boomer had plenty of practical experience in bridge-building, they thought it prudent to disguise their youth behind luxuriant whiskers. Opening an office in the Windy City, they prepared to build bridges for any railroad company that was in need of their services.

Stone and Boomer quickly established a dock and bridge yard on the Chicago River. Brother Amasa Stone contracted to build the railroad to Milwaukee, which gave Andros and Lucius a good start. Soon the lines projected to Galena,

268. *Andros B. Stone*

269. *Lucius B. Boomer*

270. *George B. Boomer*

271. *James M. Boomer*

Rock Island, Alton and to southern Illinois. All realized that they must have Howe-truss bridges, too. Stone & Boomer's Chicago yard and shops received and processed 3,500,000 feet of timber for bridges during the first year of operation.

Beyond the Mississippi, a new Pacific line and the Iron Mountain railroad were projected to serve Missouri. To tap this business, Stone & Boomer brought the latter's younger brother George out from Massachusetts to open a St. Louis branch of the firm. The precocious "baby" of the family, George Boomer had begun school at three and eventually nearly ruined his eyes with omnivorous study at Worcester Academy. Ambitious but afflicted, the student had to leave the academic world, but seized the chance to become a bridge contractor and businessman in Missouri. There was only one small drawback. When George Boardman Boomer arrived in St. Louis in February, 1852, he was all of nineteen years old.

A conservative city in which newcomers,

especially those who had not yet attained their majority, were received with dignified indifference, St. Louis cold-shouldered young George. Of his difficulties he wrote, ". . . for a man to be too young and short, too, oh combination of evils! I cannot impress upon the minds of these people that I am the man who has charge of the building of bridges for the State of Missouri."

Since Stone & Boomer held contracts with the state-subsidized Pacific Railroad, the youthful branch manager persisted. From the Federal Government he bought an entire township covered with virgin oak timber, located on the Osage River in the central part of the state. Here Boomer erected a huge saw mill for the preparation of bridge timbers, and to house the workers he established a frontier town modeled on a New England community. The founder gave the name "Castle Rock" to the place.

Little George managed to infuse a spirit of Yankee independence and industry into his little town, which was more commonly called "Boomer's Mills." He grew a wisp of a mustache, and eventually even the St. Louisians relented and accepted him. Within a year of his arrival in Missouri, Andros Stone and Lucius Boomer made George a full partner in their enterprises.

In addition to the preparation of bridge timbers for shipment to three states, Boomer had his men building houses, steamboats, wagons and furniture at Castle Rock. Not content, this "small tornado of a man" acquired another 3000 acres of pine and mineral lands in Washington County, Missouri; the wood alone was valued at $50,000. Busily commuting from St. Louis to Castle Rock and then Potosi, George Boomer lamented that it was difficult to find good bridge builders and foremen for the various jobs, "especially some of those prompt, energetic, enterprising characters raised in the cold rugged climate of New England, where a man must work or starve."

Often a distant relative, recruited to bridge-building, proved to be just that sort of character. Such was cousin James Boomer, only a year older than George, who had come West in 1849 with the intention of acquiring a farm near Bristol, Illinois.

What was termed "a disappointment in love" turned Jim Boomer from farmer to bridge builder for a while. The young lady back in Massachusetts who he hoped would share his life on the prairie married his best friend. Jim sold his crops and implements and went to Chicago, where he got work with Stone & Boomer at $1.25 per day.

Boomer was not a drinking man. In the raw construction camps of the Rock Island Railroad west of the city he was at first derided, but then gradually admired and accepted as "the only steady hand." He worked at everything. One season's jobs might include inspection of timber at the Saginaw and Detroit docks in Michigan, supervising the erection of Howe-truss bridges on muddy river banks in southern Illinois, or helping George Boomer with the haulage of prepared timber through sleepy old Potosi, Missouri. Jim quickly rose to the position of journeyman superintendent, but still yearned for the farm. After four and a half years of strenuous bridge-building he left it to have another try at Illinois sod-busting, this time with a local girl he happily acquired for a wife.

During the 1850's Stone & Boomer erected bridges on twenty-four different railroads in Illinois, Wisconsin and Missouri. Their work covered all the lines fanning out from Chicago and St. Louis, plus numerous spans for the Mississippi & Missouri Railroad in Iowa, and those of the western division of the Ohio & Mississippi Railroad between Vincennes, Indiana and Illinoistown (now East St. Louis), Illinois.

Their most famous and important contract was for the Rock Island Bridge connecting Rock

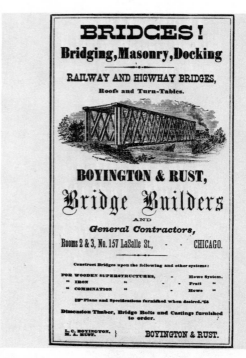

272. *Advertisement for mass-production and erection of "railway and highway bridges."*

Island, Illinois, and Davenport, Iowa. The first bridge of any kind to be built across the Mississippi River, it was to figure prominently in the sometimes violent competition between fire canoe and iron horse.

Undertaken by the "Railroad Bridge Company" formed especially for the purpose, the crossing was a natural link-up between the Chicago & Rock Island Railroad and Iowa's Mississippi & Missouri, already building toward Des Moines. Using a river survey made by Lieutenant Robert E. Lee in 1837, the company's engineer, Benjamin B. Brayton, plotted out the bridge as a segment of a looping curve of rail line. It arced over the slough at the south, across the western tip of Rock Island, and then straight across the main channel of the Mississippi at its narrowest point below the rapids.

One would think that such a grand undertaking—the first bridging of the Father of Waters—might be met by much attention and weekly accounts of progress. There was attention all right, but it consisted of the outraged howls of packet masters and river boatmen, who saw a threat to commerce along their ancient water-

273. *Stone & Boomer's Rock River Bridge on the Rock Island line in Illinois.*

BRIDGE OVER ROCK RIVER, CHICAGO AND ROCK ISLAND RAILROAD.

274. *1858 engraving shows original Rock Island bridge, first to be built across the Mississippi River.*

275. *Lucius Boomer in 1870 was willing to build both wooden and iron bridges on both Howe and Post's patents.*

276. Portion of first Rock Island Bridge of 1856-66 with suspension chains added for reinforcement.

way. Further lamentations came from St. Louis, whose businessmen pictured the diversion of Iowa trade eastward to Chicago. These vigorous protests were joined by others from people who deemed that Rock Island, site of a fort in the Black Hawk War, was government property and should not be encroached upon. It all led to a new survey of Rock Island Rapids by none other than Colonel Stephen H. Long of the Army Topographical Engineers, who probably fervently wished that one of his patent bridges could be the first across the mighty Mississippi. With commendable impartiality, he neither condemned nor approved of the site, and simply marked the proposed location for the crossing on his maps.

Despite all the vociferous opposition, the Railroad Bridge Company went ahead. The first stone of the first pier was laid September 6, 1854, the masonry work being done by John Warner of Rock Island. Stone & Boomer, who had been building Howe-truss bridges for the Rock Island line clear across Illinois, were awarded the contract for the superstructure of the Mississippi crossing.

The original plans for the bridge show a through truss design based on Howe's 1846 patent, with double arches to provide extra strength and rigidity. The main river channel crossing was composed of five fixed spans, each 250 feet in the clear, plus an arched draw of 286 feet, at that time the longest of its type in the United States. Total truss length added up to 1581 feet, to which could be added the three 150-foot clear spans over the slough, by which the railroad continued on from the south side of Rock Island to curve west again.

It is interesting to note that from the beginning it was planned to weatherboard and roof the bridge, and the original specifications called for

this. They were drawn up by Stone & Boomer's new draftsman, Moritz Lassig, a German-born engineering-school graduate who had just emigrated to America in search of greater opportunities. Later he was to become a top iron-bridge builder in his own right.

Under the direction of L. C. Boyington, who set up a branch office in Davenport, Stone & Boomer went quietly about the work of erecting the bridges over the Mississippi. Construction of stone piers, abutments and then the wooden trusses consumed nineteen months. The builders had as many as 150 men working at once on the bridges, with Jim Boomer on hand to see to some of the raising and securing of trusses.

The river boatmen and St. Louis interests tried in vain for an injunction that would halt the work. Even before the big bridge was fully completed it had a narrow escape.

On April 5, 1856 the new Louisville packet *Effie Afton*, on her first trip up the Mississippi, docked overnight at Rock Island. Next morning she sideswiped a ferry boat, but continued on upstream under reduced power and with one paddlewheel improperly operating. At the bridge she entered the 120-foot open channel on the Illinois side and got into further difficulties. Somehow the vessel managed to hit the piers on both sides and then came around broadside to ground below the short pier of the draw. Supposedly in sinking condition, the *Afton* lay there for an hour while her crew and passengers removed baggage, cargo and themselves. Then a fire in the bake shop inexplicably blazed up, consumed the wrecked steamer and burned off a full span of the nearly finished bridge. All the boats tied up on the Rock Island levee set up a jubilant din of whistling.

Laboring like demons, Stone & Boomer's crews had a new span up within two weeks. On April 21 the locomotive "Des Moines" trundled safely across from Illinois to Iowa to open the bridge for service.

Completion of this vital link in transcontinental transportation normally would have called for fireworks and the ringing of church bells, but the railroad squelched the efforts of a Davenport committee that planned to stage such a celebration. The loss of the *Effie Afton* had stirred up a new wave of indignation from the advocates of

The Romance of Western Trails

277. *Artist's conception shows Abraham Lincoln and young Ben Brayton conferring on Mississippi River currents from the Rock Island Bridge.*

river supremacy, and her owners brought suit against the bridge company.

Defendants in the celebrated case were represented by a forty-eight-year old lawyer from Springfield, Illinois, Abraham Lincoln. Before the trial opened, a special Rock Island car took him for a personal visit to the bridge. Here Lincoln conferred with railroad and construction experts who supplied him with facts and figures. Anxious to see for himself, the lanky lawyer had young Ben Brayton, son of the company's engineer, take him out on the deck of the bridge and describe the various currents and eddies which were purported to flow in the dark river below.

The information thus gained stood Lincoln well at the subsequent trial, held in Chicago early in September, 1857. Dozens of river pilots and boatmen told of their difficulties in negotiating the newly constricted channel. Then Lincoln, his bony arms flailing as he drove home his points, warmed up to his case.

"This bridge," he said, "must be treated with respect in this court, and is not to be kicked about with contempt."

Point by point, he proceeded to show quite conclusively that the *Effie Afton*'s pilot had grossly bungled the job of taking his vessel up the channel. Currents or no, the steamer had banged into piers on both sides of the passage no less than three times in a space of some 350 feet. The Springfield lawyer concluded his summation with remarks on public transportation in general, and a suggestion to both river and railroad factions to "live and let live." He referred to the height of one of the Ohio River bridges with an Irish dialect story that had both the judge and jurors in stitches.

Abraham Lincoln's efforts in the *Effie Afton* case (*Hurd et al.* vs *Railroad Bridge Company*) were successful. The jury disagreed as to whether or not the bridge constituted an obstruction to the navigation of the Mississippi. Eventually the action was dismissed and new suits were instituted by other allegedly aggrieved parties.

Although it has been widely recounted that the wreck of the *Effie Afton* was a deliberate attempt, instigated by the river interests, to get rid of the bridge, close examination of the evidence seems to indicate that the incident was an accident, pure and simple. The origin of the subsequent fire, however, is open to question.

Later events were not as innocent, and included a number of outright sabotage attempts originated by no less a body than the St. Louis Chamber of Commerce. During a three-year period, eight boats were lost in negotiating the disputed draw span and seventeen badly damaged. It was true that Benjamin Brayton had not located the big center pier exactly in line with the flow of the current, and extreme caution had to be exercised by the pilots who nosed their charges through the narrow confines of the resulting channel.

Stone & Boomer's original plans to roof and weatherboard the Rock Island Bridge proved impractical in view of the continued controversy regarding the site and the vulnerability of the structure to possible sabotage and fire.

As the weight of rolling stock increased, auxiliary suspension cables were strung along the trusses of the fixed spans. By 1866 the bridge had become too light, and the original wooden superstructure was replaced by a completely new set of trusses on the Howe plan, built with arched top chords. Again, because of the dangers of incendiarism, the covering was omitted.

During the Civil War the government resumed its title to Rock Island and established first a stockade for Confederate prisoners, and later a new arsenal on the property. Though in constant use, the railroad bridge was finally condemned by army engineers, who compromised with the

278. *Second wooden Rock Island Bridge had unusual
arched upper chords for massive Howe trusses.*

railroad in selecting a new site. In order to fully
utilize the island, a new jointly financed combination rail and wagon-road bridge of iron was
built on a more direct crossing in 1872.

An exceedingly useful bone of contention link-
ing East and West, the old Rock Island railroad
bridge and its approaches were then completely
removed. The long disputed channel passage was
cleared. In the sixteen years of litigation which
formed a noisy backdrop to its existence, the
crossing left its impact on federal laws and regu-
lations and was the direct instrument which
brought about the present jurisdiction of the
War Department over navigable waters. Today
only a fragment of one abutment remains standing on the grounds of the Rock Island Arsenal,
with a bronze plaque to make note of its historical importance.

Some of the lawsuits involving the Rock Island
Bridge called for expert testimony from the nation's leading engineers. Among those asked for
an opinion was Daniel Craig McCallum, one of
the leading railroad-bridge builders of the 1850's.

279. *Daniel C. McCallum*

A burly Scotsman with a curly beard, McCallum
had served as a bridge carpenter, foreman and
general superintendent of the Erie Railroad back
East. There in 1851 he devised and patented
"McCallum's Inflexible Arched Truss," a bridge
primarily for railroads. An exceptionally adequate design, the McCallum truss featured an
arched upper chord and stiff bracing which
pressed out from funnel-shaped iron shoes anchored in the masonry of abutments and piers.

The success of his brainchild led McCallum to
form his own company to promote its use and
erection. Specimens of the type were built not
only in the United States and Canada, but in
Panama and even Australia.

In the Middle West, one of the chief users of
the McCallum Inflexible was the broad-gauge
Ohio & Mississippi Railroad. On this line over a
hundred of the type were built during 1854–59,
varying in length from 35 to 210 feet clear spans.
The Ohio & Mississippi thought highly of their
strength, and ample proof was provided by an
accident which occurred in March 1858 at a
span over Laughery Creek west of Lawrenceburg, Indiana. On the downgrade, an engine
jumped the track about 300 feet from the bridge.
It continued on at high speed to lodge itself
within the structure, followed by the baggage
coach and two passenger cars. A block and falls
strung across the curved top chords of the
bridge was used to sort out the mess, and the
span was soon back in service. No mention seems
to have been made of the human participants in
this pileup.

In another Ohio & Mississippi mishap, a head-
on collision in a McCallum bridge stacked two
locomotives and six cars on up through the roof.
The laconic report on this spectacular cornfield
meet states: "No timbers were broken, nor was
any injury done to the bridge."

The O & M appears to have been accident-
prone during its pioneer days. Still another Mc-
Callum bridge is recalled because of its resiliency
in the face of disaster: a four-spanner plus draw
over the Wabash River at Vincennes, Indiana.
In this instance, the disabled cargo steamer
Crescent, with 800 tons of freight aboard, struck
a breakwater and then swung around in a seven-
mile current. Her bow struck with full force on
the middle span of the O & M bridge. Under

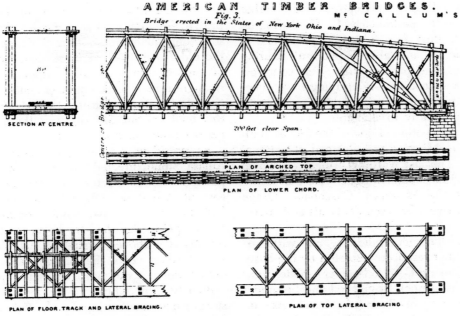

280. *Details of the McCallum patent truss for railroad use.*

this impact two lower chords snapped, but trains were running over the bridge again the same day.

McCallum's "inflexible" was a good bridge, but reverted to the difficulty of erection by ordinary builders which had hindered the development of Colonel Long's truss some years previously. On the western division of the Ohio & Mississippi, Jim Boomer's crews threw up the easier-to-build Howe trusses, enabling the line to be pushed through more speedily to East St. Louis. The high point for Daniel McCallum and his bridges was reached in a 1400-foot structure of seven spans, plus a 300-foot draw, built for the Chicago & Northwestern Railroad over the Mississippi River at Clinton, Iowa.

Like other enterprises, bridge-building languished during the Civil War, with the emphasis placed on destruction rather than construction. Daniel McCallum joined the Union cause as head of the U. S. Military Railroads. With the rank of major general he saw to it that the troops had their lines of communication in good shape, or quickly replaced if destroyed.

After a fire destroyed their bridge yard in Chicago, Stone and Boomer had dissolved their partnership in 1857. Andros Stone went into the iron business in Cleveland, a line of work already locally dominated by his well-to-do brother Amasa.

In Missouri, little George Boomer's strong anti-slavery feelings caused him to give up his bridge work and other business interests. In the face of border-state opposition he raised a regiment of 1000 men called the 26th Missouri Volunteers, and led them into action at the siege of Vicksburg. Late in the afternoon of May 22, 1863 Colonel Boomer was killed instantly by a Confederate sharpshooter's bullet. In recognition of the personal sacrifice and outstanding devotion he had given to the Union cause, he was posthumously appointed a brigadier general.

Robust Lucius Boomer resolutely carried on alone and rebuilt the bridge business in time to be of use to the Union's military rebuilders. With the endorsement of General McCallum, he received contracts for erecting railroad bridges in Tennessee, Alabama and Georgia. He even inveigled cousin Jim Boomer back off the farm to see to their erection. On some of the jobs,

Lucius was loosely associated with other Howe-truss men, particularly L. C. Boyington and Henry A. Rust. Burt & McNary of Cleveland were still active and also helped out. During some of the busy periods their joint contracts averaged some 2000 feet of bridging built every thirty days, with all the materials shipped south from Chicago, ready to assemble.

Even the completion of one of the Pacific Railroad's lines in Missouri was deemed of national importance. The last wartime bridges on which journeyman Jim Boomer worked were that road's crossings of the Meremec, Gasconade, Osage and Moreau rivers between St. Louis and Jefferson City.

Without his energetic guidance, and with surrounding timber resources depleted by the hasty war effort, General George Boomer's model community of Castle Rock languished and became a Missouri ghost town. Today its former site on the Osage River bottoms is difficult to determine exactly.

In other states the enterprising dynasty of the Howe-truss builders still persevered, and their product remained popular for a decade after the war. Boomer's Bridge Works of Chicago erected both Howe bridges and others on the newer combination wood-and-iron patent of S. S. Post. Another Boomer specialty was the preservative treatment of timber with zinc chloride, a process called "Burnettizing." Still full of vim, Lucius Boomer formed a stock company to build iron bridges (the original "American Bridge Company" of 1871–78), and Andros Stone came back in with him to help run it.

Working out of Toledo, Ohio, contractor T. H. Hamilton erected Howe-truss railroad bridges exclusively. Even the rival Smith Bridge Company of the same city would as readily take a contract for a Howe bridge as for one of their own special patent design.

It took thirty years for the ever popular Howe bridge to be gradually superseded by iron trusses of other types. The coup de grace was administered by the failure of a bridge which should never have been built.

In Cleveland, only fourteen years after first coming to Ohio, Amasa Stone became president of the prosperous Lake Shore Railroad, and the city's first millionaire. With justifiable confidence,

he still considered himself an unchallengeable bridge designer, and in 1863 he sketched out something of an innovation. This was basically the old Howe truss of more than twenty years of success, but with all components made of wrought iron. A hired engineer ventured to question the wisdom of using the new material in this manner, but Mr. Stone withered his mild remonstrance with an icy stare.

As president of the Lake Shore, autocratic Amasa Stone directed that the new bridge replace a wooden structure over the deep gulf just east of Ashtabula, Ohio. Stretching some 150 feet between massive stone abutments, "Mr. Stone's pet bridge" had tracks on the deck about seventy feet above the shallow Ashtabula River. For thirteen years the bridge carried all the heavy traffic of the railroad's main line.

Shortly after Christmas in 1876 a northeast storm came howling in off Lake Erie and began piling snow all along the Ohio shore. Westbound out of Buffalo came the Pacific Express, a doubleheader with eleven cars full of holiday travelers. In sight of Ashtabula the train rounded a bend and pulled slowly out on the iron bridge. Suddenly engineer Dan McGuire in the lead locomotive heard a thunderous report and felt the span sink beneath him.

Frantically, McGuire gave his engine full throttle and gained the west bank. Behind him the drawbar broke and the second engine dropped from sight in a wreath of smoke and steam. Unbelieving, McGuire watched helplessly as car after car shot out into space to plummet into the icy gorge below.

Of the 157 people aboard the train, only one survived the plunge and subsequent fire without injury. Eight-three were killed, drowned or burned to death on the spot.

Long months later a coroner's jury placed some of the blame on Amasa Stone for "an experiment that ought not to have been tried." In the nation's mind a "Howe truss" became synonymous with "the Ashtabula horror." Public opinion turned against him, and his money was of little use to Amasa Stone except to provide help and education for others. Six years after the disaster, plagued with sleepless nights, he took his own life.

Despite this tragedy, many specimens of the

281. *Lake Shore Railroad crossing at Ashtabula, Ohio. The ill-fated bridge which doomed Amasa Stone and, eventually, the Howe truss design.*

Howe bridge endured on Middle Western railroads until recent years.

Indiana's last covered railroad bridge was partially flood wrecked, and then torn down in 1937. A 600-foot four-span crossing of the West Fork of White River at Elliston, it carried the Bedford and Bloomfield branch of the Monon Railroad for over sixty years. Responsible for the erection of this lengthy specimen was the famous Hoosier builder Joseph J. Daniels of Rockville. During its twilight years, railroaders called the bridge "Old Nellie." Just prior to abandonment, Monon crews would let their freights clank slowly through the long wooden tunnel. On the farther shore the prudent engineer would swing aboard. He had already walked across. It seems that "Old Nellie" was of a vanishing breed, and not quite to be trusted.

282. *Burlington Railroad covered bridge near Rockport, Illinois, survived to feel the weight of diesel locomotives.*

283. The last active covered wooden railroad bridge in the Middle West stood on a branch line of the CB&Q near New Canton, Illinois, until 1951.

The only covered bridges of record in the state of Nebraska were built to serve the Chicago, Burlington & Quincy Railroad. During the period 1879–1908 there were three over the Blue River, two north and east of Seward and another west of Milford.

Longer lived were a pair of Burlington covered bridges in west-central Illinois. An 86-foot Howe truss at Hortons over Dutch Creek stood from 1887 to 1946. Nearby, spanning Kizer Creek, was a similar structure at New Canton. When the Burlington's branch line at this point was abandoned and torn up in 1951, the last covered railroad bridge not only in Illinois but in all the Middle West went with it.

Today, less than twenty covered bridges still serve the railroads of the United States, divided among the states of Vermont, New Hampshire, Washington and Oregon. In the Middle West only one such bridge has a claim on the distinction. This is the retired span at Hamilton, Illinois. Originally built as a combination wagon road and railway structure, on its present site it served highway travel for eighty-five years. Notably high-trussed and commodious, it is the last of its kind to have once known the billowing of smoke among its rafters and heard the squeal of flanged iron wheels on T-rails.

284. Closed off but preserved covered bridge at Hamilton, Illinois, is the only such structure remaining in Mid-America to have once seen use by railroad traffic.

APPENDIX I – WHAT MAKES A BRIDGE

The following is a summary of two chapters from *Covered Bridges of the Northeast*, published in 1957 as the first volume in a projected series on America's great wooden bridges and their builders.   R. S. A.

A bridge is defined simply as a structure erected to furnish a roadway over a depression or an obstacle; that is, over valleys or chasms, over water or other roads.

In general, bridges are supported in four ways: they are 1) propped from below—as by piling or trestles bedded in the bottom of a river or a defile; 2) carried for short distances by their own rigidity—as by stout logs, steel girders or prestressed concrete slabs; 3) held by the action of triangular (plus sometimes curved) arrangements of wooden or metal members, pressing against themselves as they press against land masses—as by trusses, or 4) hung from towers or upward projecting land masses—as in suspension bridges.

This book is concerned with the third classification, that of *truss* bridges. To understand them, though, it is necessary to start with the simple *stringer* crossings of the first group.

Man's first bridge was a stringer: he simply felled a tree growing on a riverbank so that it spanned the gap to the opposite bank. Then he teetered across it. Later he refined his invention by placing another log parallel to the first one and laying billets of wood across both of them to form a wider walkway, thus:

But what if a stream was wide? The longer the logs, the more likely they were to sag. The answer, developed centuries ago in Central Europe, was to cut two logs, press their butts into the banks (the shore foundations, called *abutments*) so that they met at an obtuse angle under the midpoint of the stringers; these were *braces*. Later a parallel stringer was added to close the open side of the triangle and keep the arms of the braces from shifting. The new stringer below was called the *lower chord;* the original one was the *upper chord.*

This combination of chords and braces was the first truss: a triangular system of timbers so devised that each member helped to support another, and together they supported whatever weight was put upon the whole.

Bridge building developed with piecemeal innovations during the Dark Ages, culminating in a virtually slipproof support when a centerpost was introduced to reach from the apex of the triangle to the midpoint of the lower chord, and so form this *kingpost* truss:

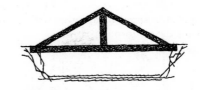

The kingpost was the earliest formal bridge truss design and it employed a primary engineering principle: a triangle will hold its shape under a load until its side members or its joints are crushed.

It is well to stop here and emphasize that the actual bridge consists of two trusses, one on each side; therefore the roadway—and, in covered spans, the roof and weatherboarding—has little to do with the bridge's basic structural efficiency. The description can be streamlined further by the reasonable practice of including the two sides in referring to the truss of a bridge.

The first kingpost truss was built under the stringers (forming a *deck* truss), where it was highly vulnerable to flood and ice. Then some inspired builder realized that kingpost triangles were equally effective when erected above the stringers (making a *through* truss). This rather oversimplified diagram and its explanation tell why:

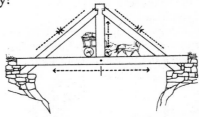

Although seemingly inelastic, the diagonal braces—called *compression members*—are subjected to squeeze as a load passes over the bridge. Meanwhile the same native flexibility allows the centerpost and lower chord—the *tension members*—to be pulled downward. So, if its truss is abutted properly into the banks, a bridge shoves harder against the land with the more weight that is put upon it, and the interaction of its truss members actually makes it stronger when it carries a load.

The whole matter of shifts and variations in stress is extremely complex and wasn't described fully until 1847. By then the wooden truss had undergone many elaborations.

A natural development was this *queenpost* truss, in which the peak of the kingpost triangle was replaced by a horizontal crosspiece to allow the base to be longer and span wider streams:

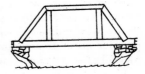

The next amplification produced the even longer *multiple kingpost,* a series of uprights with all braces inclined toward the centerpost:

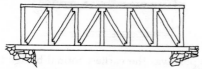

A river that was neither too swift nor too deep could be crossed by supporting such an elongated truss with one or more natural or man-made piers rising from the streambed. In a *multi-span* bridge of this sort the number of spans is one more than the number of intermediate supports between abutments.

Still, sometimes the character of a river made piers impossible: then a corollary design was used which combined an arch with a multiple kingpost. The earliest known drawings of the basic multiple kingpost and arch combinations were published in 1570 by Andrea Palladio. By that time, too, builders had begun to side and roof their bridges, simply to prevent the wooden trusses from rotting.

From the mid-1500's until the nineteenth century wooden bridge design lay dormant. Then came America's trio of pioneer builders—Palmer, Burr and Wernwag—to use the arch and kingpost for spans of a size hitherto undreamed of.

Timothy Palmer's design, patented in 1797, had auxiliary trusswork digging deep into the face of the abutments below the braced double arch:

PALMER

This was his general plan for the nation's first covered bridge, finished at Philadelphia in 1805.

A year earlier, Theodore Burr had patented this arch-truss:

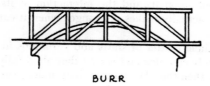

BURR

Each of its sides was a great arch sandwiched between two conventional kingpost arrangements, and its roadway, unlike Palmer's, was level. Burr used this plan for his all-time record single span (360' 4") at McCall's Ferry, Pennsylvania.

Flared kingposts bracing a double arch were the hallmarks of the best of Lewis Wernwag's many designs, which began with The Colossus in 1812. The one most popularly accepted looked like this:

WERNWAG

A wholly American truss plan appeared in 1820, ideal for cheap, strong bridges that were easy to build. It was this "lattice mode" by Ithiel Town:

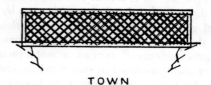

TOWN

Merely a series of overlapping triangles with no arches or uprights, it resembled a crisscross garden fence that could be "built by the mile and cut off by the yard" to support spans up to 200 feet in length. It was his new approach to the use of the basic unadorned triangle that made Town's truss unique.

A decade later Col. Stephen H. Long introduced this panel truss, a series of boxed X's with three or more panels comprising the entire truss:

LONG

In 1840 William Howe brought about a bridge building revolution by introducing an iron rod into wooden trusses. Howe's design unabashedly copied the Long panel, replacing its uprights with iron tie-rods that could be readily adjusted with nuts and turnbuckles:

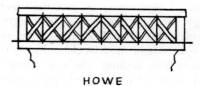

HOWE

Thus he coped with the major weakness of wood in bridge construction: the elasticity which allows strength-giving compression also permits the joints of an upright tension member to pull apart under heavy loads.

The Howe truss became the favored railroad bridge across America, and even influenced bridge construction in Europe and Asia. With it, wooden bridge building reached its peak; and with it the transition was made to bridges built of iron and steel.

APPENDIX II -- *Tabulation of Existing Covered Bridges*

Recent years have brought a great proliferation of newly built covered bridges. These range from tiny stringer spans in private back-yard gardens to highway department-constructed replicas of concrete and steel, on which are superimposed purely ornamental wooden timbers and roofs.

Of these last, there are notable full-size spans at Lake of the Woods State Park in Illinois and the Sleepy Hollow development near Sylvania, Ohio. Still another is in Mohican State Park near Loudonville, Ohio. To an extent, this trend is admirable. There is, however, an increasing danger of overlooking the merits of actual and authentic covered bridges, whose continued existence would seem a far more worthy cause.

Among both groups and individual covered-bridge fanciers and "collectors," the inclusion of new and "garden variety" covered bridges in various listings is generally considered to be of dubious value. This is not simply "buff" snobbery. In addition to full-size authentic spans whose weathered timbers have seen the passage of a full century or more, some tabulations include things like a "quaint olde bridge" with no trusswork stretched flat on dry land, or a pagoda-like passage for pedestrians, reaching all of six feet across a drainage ditch. This leads to disappointment by serious seekers who may have traveled untold miles to view one of these monstrosities.

We have chosen with few exceptions to enumerate only full-sized covered bridges, which are or were authentic highway crossings. In general, the building period of "old" covered bridges ends with the second decade of the present century.

This list is accurate and complete as far as compilation has been currently possible. In the fast-changing world of covered bridges there will quickly be deletions, corrections and even an occasional addition.

R.S.A.

2/26/68

LOCATION	NAME	OWNER	STREAM	Spans & Length	DATE	TYPE	BUILDER, etc.
ILLINOIS							
BUREAU COUNTY							
2 Mi No of Princeton	Red		Big Bureau Creek	1 —93	1863	Howe	
HANCOCK COUNTY							
Hamilton			Slough of Mississippi River	1 — 169	1869	Howe	Orig. part of Mississippi River Bridge. Relocated here in 1882
HENDERSON COUNTY							
2 Mi No of Gladstone	Eames	RP	Henderson Creek	1 —102	1865 Possibly 1845-46	Burr	
KNOX COUNTY							
7 Mi NW of Douglas	Wolf		Spoon River	1 —106	1874	Howe	
RANDOLPH COUNTY							
4 Mi E of Chester		RP	Little Mary's River	1 — 80	1854	Burr	
SANGAMON COUNTY							
4 Mi W of Springfield			Spring Creek	1 — 60	1883	Burr	
N W of Glenarm			Sugar Creek	1 — 52	c.1880	Burr	
SHELBY COUNTY							
2 Mi NE of Cowden	Thompson Mill		Kaskaskia River	1 —110	c.1868	Howe	
WARREN COUNTY							
2 Mi SW of Greenbush			Swan Creek	1 — 58	c.1880	Queenpost	
INDIANA							
ADAMS COUNTY							
NE of Geneva	Ceylon		Wabash River	1 —126	1860	Howe	
BARTHOLOMEW COUNTY							
Columbus	Mill Race Park			1 —145		Howe	Moved from orig. site 2 Mi E of Columbus over Clifty Creek, 1966
1½ Mi SW of Taylorsville	Tanney Hill		Driftwood River	1 —236	1870	Howe	

LOCATION	NAME	OWNER	STREAM	Spans & Length	DATE	TYPE	BUILDER, etc.
BROWN COUNTY							
Brown Co. State Park	Ramp Creek		Salt Creek	1 — 96	1838	Burr Double Lane	Aaron Wolf. Originally built 1838 over Ramp Cr., near Fincastle, Putnam Co. Moved here 1932
CARROLL COUNTY							
NE of Cutler	Adams Mill		Wild Cat Creek	1—144	1873	Howe w/Aux.arch	Indianapolis Bridge Co.
NE of Owasco	Lancaster or Beard		Wild Cat Creek	1—133	1870	Howe	
DEARBORN COUNTY							
Guilford		RP		1—104	1879	Burr	A.M.Kennedy & 2 Sons, to be re-erected in Park
DE KALB COUNTY							
Spencerville			St. Joseph River	1—160	1875	Howe	George Woerntz & Son
NE of Spencerville	Coburn		St. Joseph River	1—154	1869	Howe	George Woerntz & Son, to be replaced
So. of St.Johns	Cedar Chapel	P	(Cedar Creek)	1—110	1884	Howe	On dry land
FAYETTE COUNTY							
NE of Glenwood	Longwood		Williams Creek	1— 92	1884	Burr	Kennedy Bros.
FOUNTAIN COUNTY							
Wallace			Sugar Mill Creek	1— 81	1871	Howe	
SW of Veedersburg	Cade's Mill		Coal Creek	1—150	1854	Howe	Capt. White Later rebuilding?
Rob Roy			Big Shawnee Cr.	1—120	1860	Howe	
FRANKLIN COUNTY							
Fairfield			East Fk. Whitewater River	2—300	1866	Howe	To be removed for flood control proj.
1 Mi So of Brookville	Lower Blue Creek	A	Blue Creek	1—130	1894	Howe	
4 Mi W of Oldenburg			Salt Creek	1— 92	1887	Howe	
4½ Mi E of Oldenburg	Haymond		Pipe Creek	1—115	1881	Howe	
5 Mi So of Mt. Carmel	Snow Hill		Johnsons Fork	1— 75		Howe	
Metamora	Aqueduct		Duck Creek	1— 83	1846	Burr	Covered Wooden Aqueduct for Whitewater Canal, rebuilt 1946-49
GIBSON COUNTY							
3½ Mi SW of Crawleyville	Red		Big Bayou	1—170	1875	Smith	
6 Mi NE of Princeton	Moore's		Patoka River	1—150	1876	Smith	W. T. Washer
Wheeling			Patoka River	1—163	1877	Smith	W. T. Washer
GRANT COUNTY							
Mathews	New Cumberland		Mississinewa R	1—167	1879	Smith	Smith Bridge Co. Washed away 1913 & returned
GREENE COUNTY							
1½ Mi S of Bloomfield			Richland Creek	1—100	1883	Burr	A.M.Kennedy & Sons
HOWARD COUNTY							
Kokomo	Highland Park or Vermont		Kokomo Creek	1—102	1874	Smith	Moved here from Wildcat Creek at Vermont 1958
JACKSON COUNTY							
NW of Brownstown	Ewing		East Fork White River	1—350	1870	Howe	J. J. Daniels
2½ Mi NE of Brownstown	Shieldstown		East Fork White River	2—331	1876	Burr	J. J. Daniels
Medora			East Fork White River	3—434	1875	Burr	J. J. Daniels
1½ Mi NW of Seymour	Bells Ford	A	East Fork White River	2—325	1869	Post	Robert Patterson
JENNINGS COUNTY							
Scipio			Sand Creek	1—140	1886	Howe	Smith Bridge Co. Moved here from unknown location
7 Mi S of Vernon			Graham River	1—123	1887	Daniel Baron	
LAKE COUNTY							
Crown Point	Fairground Park			1— 85	1878	Burr	A. M. Kennedy & Sons Orig."Shelhorn Bridge" 2 Mi. So. of Milroy in Rush Co., moved here 1933
LAWRENCE COUNTY							
W of Williams			East Fork White River	2—376	1884	Howe	J. J. Daniels

LOCATION	NAME	OWNER	STREAM	Spans & Length	DATE	TYPE	BUILDER, etc.
MARION COUNTY							
Traders Point	Brown Farm		Pond	1 — 88	1882	Howe	Josiah Durfee. Orig. built over Fishback Creek on 86th St. Moved here 1960
MONROE COUNTY							
3 Mi No. of Bloomington	Milligan		Bean Blossom Cr.	1—115	1879	Howe	To be re-located?
MONTGOMERY COUNTY							
Darlington			Sugar Creek	2—166	1867-68	Howe	Joseph Kress
N E of Shades St. Park	Deer's Mill		Sugar Creek	2—275	1878	Burr	J. J. Daniels
MORGAN-PUTNAM COUNTIES							
3 Mi N W of Eminence	Parker		Mill Creek	1—120	1886	Howe	
OWEN COUNTY							
Cataract	Cataract Falls		Mill Creek	1—140	1876	Smith	
OWEN-PUTNAM COUNTIES							
N W of Quincy	Sharpe or County Line		Mill Creek	1—100	1915	Burr	J. A. Britton
PARKE COUNTY							
1 Mi S.E. of Mansfield			Rocky Fork	1— 72	1900	Burr	J. J. Daniels
2 Mi S W of Mansfield	Connelly Ford		Big Raccoon Creek	1—192	1906	Burr	J. P. Van Fossen
2 Mi S W of Bridgeton	Jeffries Ford		Big Raccoon Creek	2—204	1915	Burr	J. A. Britton & Sons
Bridgeton			Big Raccoon Creek	2—245	1868	Burr	J. J. Daniels
No of Rockville	Nevins			1—155	1920	Burr	J. A. Britton & Son Orig. built 1920 at Catlin over Lit.Raccoon Creek, moved here
Jessup			Lt. Raccoon Creek	1—155	1910	Burr	J. P. Van Fossen
N E of Rosedale	Thorpe Ford	A	Big Raccoon Creek	1—163	1912	Burr	J. A. Britton
East of Rosedale	Red		Big Raccoon Creek	2—248	1880	Burr	J. J. Daniels
Coxville	Roseville		Big Raccoon Creek	2—263	1910	Burr	J. Brooks
N W of Coxville	Harry Evans		Iron Run	1— 65	1908	Burr	J. A. Britton
3 Mi No. of Coxville	Zacke Cox		Iron Run	1— 54	1908	Burr	J. A. Britton
Mecca		A	Big Raccoon Creek	1—150	1873	Burr	J. J. Daniels
2 Mi S E of Montezuma	Sim Smith	P	Leatherwood Creek	1— 84	1883	Burr	J. A. Britton
No of Rockville	Catlin			1— 54	1907	Burr	Clark McDaniel, Orig. built 1907 at Catlin over Sunderland Creek. Moved to Golf Course here
2½ Mi N E of Catlin	McAllister		Lt. Raccoon Creek	1—126	1914	Burr	J. A. Britton
2½ Mi S E of Rockville	Crooks		Lt. Raccoon Creek	1—132	1867	Burr	Orig. 1856, washed out-rebuilt
2 Mi E of Catlin	Neet		Lt. Raccoon Creek	1—143	1904	Burr	J. J. Daniels
1½ Mi E of Rockville	Billie Creek		Williams Creek	1— 62	1895	Burr	J. J. Daniels
Mansfield			Big Raccoon Creek	2—247	1867	Burr	J. J. Daniels
3 Mi E of Milligan	Dooley Station		Lt. Raccoon Creek	1—130	1856	Burr	Aaron Wolf, Orig. blt. 1856 at Portland Mills Moved here 1960-61
5½ Mi N E of Rockville	Adams		Lt. Raccoon Creek	1—154	1907	Burr	Frankfort Construction Co.
N W of Marshall	Beeson		Roaring Creek	1— 55	1906	Burr	Frankfort Construction Co.
2½ Mi S W of Bloomingdale	Harry Wolf		Leatherwood Cr.	1— 72	1899	Burr	J. A. Britton
2 Mi E of Montezuma	Marion		Leatherwood Cr.	1— 83	1896	Burr	J. J. Daniels
No of West Union			Sugar Creek	2—315	1876	Burr	J. J. Daniels
2½ Mi N W of Annapolis	Jackson		Sugar Creek	1—207	1861	Burr	J. J. Daniels
2 Mi S W of Tangier	Earl Ray		Mill Creek	1— 92	1907	Burr	D. M. Brown
Lodi (Waterman)	Coal Creek		Coal Creek	1—170	1869	Burr	J. J. Daniels
1½ Mi S of Tangier			Rush Creek	1— 77	1904	Burr	William Hendricks
2½ Mi S W of Tangier	Marshall		Rush Creek	1— 56	1917	Burr	J. A. Britton
3 Mi N W of Tangier	Bowsher Ford		Mill Creek	1— 72	1915	Burr	Eugene Britton
West of Turkey Run Street Park	Cox Ford		Sugar Creek	1—176	1913	Burr	J. A. Britton & Edgar Britton
N W of Turkey Run Street Park	Wilkins Mill		Sugar Mill Creek	1—102	1906	Burr	William Hendricks
Turkey Run St. Park	Narrows	A	Sugar Creek	1—121	1882	Burr	J. A. Britton
5 Mi E of Rockville	State Sanitorium		Lt.Raccoon Creek	1—154	1912	Burr	J. A. Britton
2½ Mi No of Annapolis	Jordan Farm	P	Square Rock Branch of Sugar Creek	1— 42	1897	Queenpost	Pearly Weaver

LOCATION	NAME	OWNER	STREAM	Spans & Length	DATE	TYPE	BUILDER, etc.
PERRY-SPENCER COUNTIES							
Huffman	Huffman Mills		Anderson River	1—140	1863-64	Burr	W. T. Washer
2 Mi S of Huffman	Shoals		Anderson River	1— 98	1865	Burr	W. T. Washer
PIKE COUNTY							
No of Pikeville			Patoka River	1—134	1887	Burr	W. T. Washer
PUTNAM COUNTY							
1½ Mi E of Raccoon			Cornstalk Creek	1— 82	1917	Burr	J. A. Britton
1½ Mi S E of Bainbridge	Bakers Camp		Big Walnut Creek	1—128	1901?	Burr	J. J. Daniels
2½ Mi N E of Bainbridge	Pine Bluff		Big Walnut Creek	2—211		Howe	
1½ Mi N E of Bainbridge	Rolling Stone		Big Walnut Creek	1—103	1915	Burr	J. A. Britton
S E of Clinton Falls			Little Walnut Creek	1—122	1938-39	Burr	Orig.built as double-lane at Raccoon by Aaron Wolf,1838, Moved & rebuilt at this site as single lane
1 Mi N W of Clinton Falls	Edna Collins		Little Walnut Creek	1— 80	1922	Burr	Charles Hendrix
N W of Green Castle	Dunbar		Big Walnut Creek	2—174	1880	Burr	
2½ Mi W of Limedale	Oakalla		Big Walnut Creek	1—152	1898	Burr	J. J. Daniels
3 Mi N W of Manhattan	Houk		Big Walnut Creek	2—210	1880	Howe	Massillon Bridge Co.
½ Mi S E of Manhattan			Deer Creek	1—120	1895	Burr	J. J. Daniels
3 Mi S E of Pleasant Gardens	Dick Huffman		Big Walnut Creek	2—265	1880	Howe	
5 Mi So of Pleasant Gardens	Cradle		Croys Creek	1— 71	1889	Burr	J. A. Britton
RANDOLPH COUNTY							
4 Mi W of Ridgeville	Emmetsville		Mississinewa River	1—124	1883	Burr	A. M. Kennedy & Sons
RIPLEY COUNTY							
1½ Mi N W of Holton			Otter Creek	1—112	1884	Howe	Thomas Hardman
3½ Mi N W of Milan			Ripley Creek	1— 59	1889	Howe	Philip Ensminger
East of Versailles	Busching		Laughery Creek	1—176	1885	Howe	Thomas Hardman
RUSH COUNTY							
2 Mi N E of Rushville	Smith		Big Flat Rock River	1—124	1877	Burr	A. M. Kennedy & Sons
2½ Mi N E of Arlington	Offutt's Ford		Little Blue River	1— 85	1884	Burr	Kennedy Bros.
2½ Mi N E of Moscow	Forsythe Mill		Big Flat Rock River	1—181	1888	Burr	Emmett L.Kennedy
2 Mi N E of Milroy	Winship		Little Flat Rock Cr.	1— 80	1873	Burr	A.M.Kennedy & Sons
Moscow			Big Flat Rock River	2—372	1886	Burr & Q.P.Aux	Emmett L.Kennedy
4 Mi N E of Rushville	Norris Ford		Big Flat Rock River	1—154	1916	Burr	E.L.Kennedy & Sons
SHELBY COUNTY							
N E of Shelbyville	Cedar Ford		Little Blue River	1—140	1885	Burr	Kennedy Bros.
UNION COUNTY							
Brownsville			E Fk Whitewater River	1—166	1840	Long	James Morris
Dunlapsville			E Fk Whitewater River	2—300	1870	Burr	Archibald M.Kennedy To be flooded out
VERMILLION COUNTY							
1½ Mi N W of Universal			Brouillette's Cr.	1—122	1879	Burr	J. J. Daniels
1 Mi N W of Hillsdale			Little Raccoon Cr.	1—104	1876	Burr	J. J. Daniels
1 Mi N W of Newport			Little Vermillion R.	1—180	1885	Burr	J. J. Daniels
Eugene			Big Vermillion R.	1—175	1873	Burr	J. J. Daniels
VIGO COUNTY							
3 Mi W of Riley	Erisman's or Irishman's		Honey Creek	2— 75		Queen Post Variant	
WABASH COUNTY							
Roann	Roann		Eel River	2—288	1872	Howe	Smith Bridge Co.
North Manchester			Eel River	1—150	1872	Smith	Smith Bridge Co. Has attached covered sidewalk
Dora	Dora		(Salamonie River)	1—156	1871	Howe	(?) Moved to Dora-New Holland Historical Village site.

IOWA

LOCATION	NAME	OWNER	STREAM	Spans & Length	DATE	TYPE	BUILDER, etc.
KEOKUK COUNTY							
So of Delta			No Fork Skunk River	1— 76	1869	Burr	

LOCATION	NAME	OWNER	STREAM	Spans & Length	DATE	TYPE	BUILDER, etc.
MADISON COUNTY							
5 Mi N W of Winterset	Hogback		North River	1—	1884	Town	H. P. Jones
4½ Mi N W of Bevington	Donahoe or Cutler		North River	1—	1870	Town	Eli Cox
5 Mi W of Pammel St Pk	Roseman		Middle River	1—113	1883	Town/W Queenpost	H. P. Jones
3 Mi S E of Winterset	Holliwell		Middle River	1—100	1880	Town/Arch & arched q p	H. P. Jones & G.K. Foster
10 Mi N E of Winterset	McBride		North Branch River	1—	1885	Town	J. P. Clark
3 Mi N E of Winterset	Cedar or Casper		Cedar Creek	1—	1883	Town	H. P. Jones-Orig. blt. on main highway north, moved here 1920
West of St. Charles	Imes Bridge		Clanton Creek	1—	1870	Town/W Queenpost	Orig. blt. over Middle River at Wilkins' Mill nr Patterson,moved to this site 1887
MARION COUNTY							
3 Mi S of Attica	Hammond		North Cedar Creek	1— 60	1870	Howe	
1 Mi W of Marysville			South Cedar Creek	1—	1891	Town	Orig. built 15 Mi N W of Marysville, moved here 1926. To be re-erected in Knoxville.
POLK COUNTY							
Ewing Park S E of Des Moines	Owens		Arm of Lake Easter	1—100	1888	Howe	Sam Gray Moved 1968 to present site.Formerly N E of Carlisle over old channel of North River.

MICHIGAN

LOCATION	NAME	OWNER	STREAM	Spans & Length	DATE	TYPE	BUILDER, etc.
IONIA COUNTY							
S W of Smyrna	White's		Flat River	1—120	1869	Brown	J. N. Brazee & J. H. Walker
KENT COUNTY							
Ada	Bradfield	A	Thornapple River	1—125	1866	Brown	Jared N. Brazee
North of Lowell	Fallasburg	Park	Flat River	1—100	1862	Brown	Jared N. Brazee
ST. JOSEPH COUNTY							
North of Centerville	Langley		St. Joseph River	3—282	1887	Howe	Pierce Bodner Raised 8 ft. on abutments in 1910
WAYNE COUNTY							
Dearborn	Greenfield Village		Pond	1— 75	1832	Burr	Orig. built by Joshua Ackley & Daniel Clouse in Penna. Moved here by Ford Motor Co. 1938

MISSOURI

LOCATION	NAME	OWNER	STREAM	Spans & Length	DATE	TYPE	BUILDER, etc.
CAPE GIRARDEAU COUNTY							
Burfordville	Bollinger Mill		Whitewater Creek	1—140	1867	Howe	Joseph Lansman
JEFFERSON COUNTY							
Near Goldman	LeMay Ferry Road		Sandy Creek	1— 76	1886	Howe	Henry Steffin
LINN COUNTY							
3 Mi W of Laclede		A	Old Channel Locust Creek	1—	c. 1865	Howe	
MONROE COUNTY							
3 Mi So of Paris	Union		Elk Fork, Salt River	1—	1867	Burr	Joseph Elliott
PLATTE COUNTY							
Tracy	Noah's Ark			1— 76	1878	Howe	In fairgrounds moved from N E of Platte Cty. over Little Platte River

OHIO

LOCATION	NAME	OWNER	STREAM	Spans & Length	DATE	TYPE	BUILDER, etc.
ADAMS COUNTY							
Harshaville			Cherry Fork	1—90		Mult K-P Aux Lam. Arch	
4 Mi S W of West Union	Gov. Kirker		East Fork Eagle Creek	1—66		Mult Kingpost	
ASHTABULA COUNTY							
3 Mi E of Ashtabula	Olin or Dewey Road		Ashtabula River	1—116	1875	Town/WAux. Bracing	
4 Mi N E of Kingsville	Creek Road		Conneaut Creek	1—118		Town	
4 Mi S E of Conneaut	Middle Road		Conneaut Creek	1—136	1868	Howe	

LOCATION	NAME	OWNER	STREAM	Spans & Length	DATE	TYPE	BUILDER, etc.
ASHTABULA COUNTY Continued							
2 Mi S W of Monroe Center	Root Road		Ashtabula River	1— 97	1868	Town	
2½ Mi N W of Sheffield	Benetka Road		Ashtabula River	1—115		Town	
3 Mi N W of Pierpont	Graham Road		Ashtabula River	1— 88	1913	Town W/Aux Bracing	
3½ Mi S E of Jefferson	So Denmark Road		Mill Creek	1— 85		Town	
1½ Mi N W of Jefferson	Doyle or Mullen Road		Mill Creek	1— 92	1868	Town	
Eagleville	Foreman Road		Mill Creek	1—133	1862	Town	Moved 100' to this site in 1870's
3 Mi S W of Austinburg	Mechanicsville		Grand River	1—154	1873?	Howe W/integrated arch	
Harpersfield			Grand River	2—236	1873	Howe	Mr. Potter
2½ Mi S W of Eagleville	Fobes Road		Grand River	1—118		Howe	Moved to this site in 1911 from Orwell-Windsor Rd. (now abandoned)
1½ Mi N W of Rock Creek	Riverdale Road		Grand River	1—127	1874	Town w/Aux. Bracing	
Windsor Mills	Wiswell Road		Phelps Creek	4—121		Town	
3 Mi S W of Orwell	Windsor Road		Grand River	1— 90	c.1870	Town	
ATHENS COUNTY							
1 Mi N E of Glouster	Dallas		Sunday Creek	1— 74		Mult. Kingpost	
1 Mi No of Truetown			Sunday Creek	1— 96		Howe	
2½ Mi N E of Pratts Fork			Shade Creek	1— 64		Mult. Kingpost	
BROWN COUNTY							
2 Mi No of New Hope			White Oak Creek	1—136	1878	Smith	
1 Mi S W of New Hope	Bethel Road		White Oak Creek	1—162		Howe-W/Aux. Lam. arch	
2 Mi S W of Vera Cruz	McCafferty Road		East Fork Little Miami River	1—157		Howe	
2 Mi S W of Georgetown	Columbus-Young Road		White Oak Creek	1—156	1879	Smith	
3 Mi So of Decatur			Eagle Creek	1—174	1872	Smith	
4 Mi S E of Ripley	Martins Hill		Beetle Creek	1— 96	1875	Long-W/Aux. Arch	
3½ Mi N E of Ripley	North Pole		Eagle Creek	1—156	1875	Smith	
3 Mi S E of Russellville	Geo.Miller Road		W Fk Eagle Creek	1—156	1875	Smith	
BUTLER COUNTY							
North of Oxford			Four Mile Creek	2—206	1880-85	Long	Re-built in Gov. Bebb Park near Hamilton
CLERMONT COUNTY							
3 Mi E of Perintown	Stonelick Road		Stonelick Creek	1—133	1878	Howe	
CLINTON COUNTY							
1 Mi W of Martinsville			Todd's or Little East Fork	1— 70		Mult. Kingpost	
COLUMBIANA COUNTY							
4 Mi S E of Hanoverton	Sells		West Fk Little Beaver Creek	1— 48	1878	Mult.Kingpost	Robinson & McCracken
5 Mi S E of Hanoverton	Jim McClellan		West Fk Little Beaver Creek	1— 52	c. 1870	Mult. Kingpost	
6 Mi S E of Hanoverton	McKaigs Mill		West Fk Little Beaver Creek	1— 53	c. 1870	Mult. Kingpost	
3 Mi N W of Lisbon	Teegarden or Centennial		Middle Fk Little Beaver Creek	1— 66	1876	Mult. Kingpost	
2½ Mi N of Lisbon	Miller Road		Millsite Creek	1— 22		Mult. Kingpost	
3 Mi N E of Lisbon	Church Hill Road		Middle Run	1— 19' 3"	c.1870	Kingpost	
COSHOCTON COUNTY							
3 Mi N E of Blissfield			Doughty Creek	1— 85	1867-68	Mult. Kingpost	Jonas Asire
1½ Mi E of Blissfield	Helmick		Killbuck Creek	2—166	1862-63	Mult. Kingpost	John Shrake
3 Mi S E of Conesville			Wills Creek	1—134	1879-80 1884	Mult. Kingpost Arches added 1884	Orig by F Mayer Arches by M Lapp 1884, washed out rebuilt 1884
DELAWARE COUNTY							
1½ Mi N E of Olive Green	Chambers Road		Big Walnut Creek	1— 73	1874	Childs	E. S. Sherman
FAIRFIELD COUNTY							
N W of Pickerington	Blacklick		Blacklick Creek	1—130	1888	Howe	
N E of Pickerington	Taylor		Sycamore Creek	1— 60		Mult.Kingpost	To be replaced
N E of Pickerington	Stemen House		Sycamore Creek	1— 70	1888	Howe	
N W of Baltimore	Fultz		Poplar Creek	1— 74	1891	King & Queenpost	
N W of Baltimore	Hizey		Poplar Creek	1— 77	1891	Burr	J. W. Buchanan
N W of Baltimore	Macklin House		Br of Poplar Creek	1— 65	1880	Mult.Kingpost & Lam. arch	

LOCATION	NAME	OWNER	STREAM	Spans & Length	DATE	TYPE	BUILDER, etc.
FAIRFIELD COUNTY Continued							
N E of Carroll	Jonathan Bright No 2		Poplar Creek	1 – 72	1881	Inverted Metal Arch	Hocking Valley Bridge Works
N E of Carroll	Peter Ety		Walnut Creek	1 –104	1913	Mult.Kingpost	
S E of Amanda	George Hutchins		Clear Creek	1 – 58		Kingpost	
So of Clearport	Hannaway		Clear Creek	1 – 81		Mult. Kingpost	
E of Clearport	Johnson		Clear Creek	1 – 92		Howe	
S E of Clearport	Starner or Written Rock		Clear Creek	1 –103	1891	Burr (Lam.Arch)	
E of Canal Winchester	Zeller Smith		Sycamore Creek	1 – 73	1906	Mult. Kingpost	
S E of Canal Winchester	Shade		Walnut Creek	1 –122	1871	Burr	J. W. Buchanan
S E of Canal Winchester	Charles Loucks		Walnut Creek	1 –130		Burr	J. W. Buchanan
N E of Carroll	E. B. Weaver		Walnut Creek	1 –105		Burr	
S W of Baltimore	McCleery		Walnut Creek	1 – 90	1883	Kingpost	
N W of Baltimore	Shryer or Game Farm		Br of Paw Paw Creek	1 – 65		Mult. Kingpost	On skew
N E of Thurston	Charles Holliday		Walnut Creek	1 – 92		Mult. Kingpost	
N of Rushville	Mary Ruffner		Rush Creek	1 – 78	1869	Smith	
N E of Rushville	R. F. Baker		Rush Creek	1 – 66		Mult. Kingpost	Buttressed
N E of Rush Creek	Moyer		Little Rush Creek	1 – 98	1915	Mult. Kingpost W/Lam. arch	On Skew
N W of Rush Creek	Jonathan Rabb		Br of Raccoon Creek	1 – 41	1891	Queenpost	
N E of Sugar Grove	May Hummel		Rush Creek	1 –103	1873	Smith W/Lam Arch	
N E of Clearport	Mink Hollow		Arney Run	1 – 51		Mult.Kingpost	
E of Amanda	Valentine		Muddy Prairie Run	1 – 35		Kingpost-X Center	
S of Amanda	Shaeffer-Campbell		Clear Creek	1 – 63	1891	Mult. Kingpost	
N W of Lancaster	Rock Mill		Hocking River	1 – 33		Queenpost	
N of Baltimore	Roley School		Br. of Paw Paw Cr.	1 – 45		Kingpost	Orig. spanned Canal. Moved here 1914
N E of Carroll	Jackson Ety	P	Walnut Creek	1 – 76		Mult. Kingpost	Orig. spanned Canal. Moved here 1912
FRANKLIN COUNTY							
1 Mi So of Canal Winchester	Bergstresser		Walnut Creek	1 –134	1887	Partridge	Columbus Bridge Co.
No. Grove City	Wesner		Big Run	1 – 48		Queen Post	Orig. built in Muskingum Co.,re-erected here 1967
GREENE COUNTY							
1 Mi N E of New Burlington	Cemetery		Andersons Fork	1 –128		Howe	
3 Mi N E of New Burlington	Mill Road (East)		Andersons Fork	1 –145	1852	Buckingham	
2½ Mi N E of New Burlington	Engle Mill Road (West)		Andersons Fork	1 –136	1870	Smith	
So of Yellow Springs	Jacoby Road		Little Miami River	1 –142	1869	Burr	
6 Mi N E of Xenia	Stevenson Road		Massies Creek	1 – 95	1873	Smith	
1½ Mi No of Wilberforce	Charlton Mill		Massies Creek	1 –120		Howe	E. Squire
5 Mi N W of Jamestown	Ballard Road		No Br Caesar's Creek	1 – 80		Howe	
GUERNSEY COUNTY							
3 Mi So of Birds Run	Indian Camp		Indian Camp Run	1 – 37		Mult.Kingpost	
N E of New Cumberland	Frisbee Farm	P	Buffalo Fork	1 – 40	1861	Kingpost	William T. Crow
1½ Mi S E of Quaker City	Reservoir	A	Leatherwood Creek	1 – 42	1900	Mult. Kingpost	
Cambridge	Armstrong Mill		In Park	1 – 66		Mult. Kingpost	Orig. over Salt Fork at Clio 5 Mi N E of Cambridge. Moved here 1967
HAMILTON COUNTY							
1 Mi N of Mt. Healthy	Groff Mill		West Fork,Mill Creek	2 – 45	1850?	Queenpost	Jediah Hill,Ctr. pier added.
HARRISON COUNTY							
2 Mi So of Freeport		A	Skull Creek	1 – 45		Mult.Kingpost	
6 Mi S W of Cadiz		AP	Brushy Fork	1 – 30		Queenpost	
HIGHLAND COUNTY							
3 Mi S E of Rainsboro	Barrett Mill		Rocky Fork	1 –151		Long	
JACKSON COUNTY							
4 Mi S W of Petersburg			Little Scioto River	1 – 71	1869	Smith	
Byer			Pigeon Creek	1 – 74	1872	Smith	
Buckeye Furnace			Little Raccoon Cr.	1 – 59	1872	Smith	
LAWRENCE COUNTY							
2 Mi S W of Platform			Guyan Creek	1 – 77		Queenpost	Truss of iron members
LICKING COUNTY							
3 Mi E of Croton			Otter Creek	1 – 50		Kingpost	
5 Mi S W of Fallsburg	Dunn		Br.of Rocky Fork	1 – 49	1882	Mult.Kingpost	Mr. Mercer
2 Mi N W of Fallsburg	Mercer		Wakatomica Cr.	1 – 68	1877	Mult.Kingpost	Mr. Babcock
1 Mi N W of Fallsburg	Gregg's Mill or Pine Bluff		Wakatomica Cr.	2 –126	1882	Mult.Kingpost	

LOCATION	NAME	OWNER	STREAM	Spans & Length	DATE	TYPE	BUILDER, etc.
LICKING COUNTY Continued							
1 Mi N of Fallsburg	Johnny Little or		Wakatomica Cr.	1 – 73	1877	Burr	Portions of truss removed
3 Mi S E of Johnstown	Mercer Saw Mill		Lobdell Cr.	1 – 57		Mult. Kingpost	
3 Mi N of Granville			Dry Creek	1 – 69		Mult. Kingpost	
3 Mi. N W of Newark			Dry Creek	1 – 67		Mult. Kingpost	
2½ Mi S of Hanover			Brushy Fork	1 – 52		Mult. Kingpost	
1½ Mi S of Hickman	Davis	P	Rocky Fork	1 – 50	1947	Mult. Kingpost	Ernest Davis
LOGAN COUNTY							
2 Mi S E of Bloom Center			Great Miami River	1 – 136	1876	Howe	
4 Mi N W of Huntsville	Russells Point		Great Miami River	1 – 96	1877	Howe	
MIAMI COUNTY							
1 Mi N of Troy	E. L. Dean		Great Miami River	2 – 223	1860	Long	
MONROE COUNTY							
3 Mi E of Graysville	Foraker		Little Muskingum R.	1 – 98	1877	Mult. Kingpost	
1¼ Mi N of Rinard Mills	Long		Clear Fork Creek	3 – 192		Mult. Kingpost, W/Aux. arch	
MONTGOMERY COUNTY							
Germantown			Little Twin Creek	1 – 103	1870	Inverted Iron Bowstring	Originally erected nearby Moved this site 1911
Dayton	Carillon Park	P	Miami & Erie Canal Bed	1 – 55	1948	Burr Variant (Orig. Warren)	Orig. built near Bellbrook in Greene Co.,adapted & moved here 1948
So of Germantown	Jasper Road	P	Mud Lick Creek	1 – 55	1877	Warren W/Aux.arch	Originally S.E.of New Jasper in Greene Co. Re-erected here 1966
MORGAN COUNTY							
2½ Mi N W of Bristol		P	Br. of Meigs Creek	1 – 65		Mult. Kingpost	
2 Mi N E of Chester Hill			Wolf Creek	1 – 80		Burr/W/Lam.Arch	
1½ Mi S W of Eagle Port			Island Run	1 –		Mult. Kingpost	
Reddy Killowat Campsite Park			Brannons Run	1 – 40		Mult. Kingpost	Moved from Renrock, Noble Co.to site 1965
5 Mi N W of Ringgold				1 –			
MUSKINGUM COUNTY							
4½ Mi S W of Zanesville	Coudermill Rd	P	Thompsons Run	1 – 45	1898	Kingpost	
3 Mi N W of Norwich		P	Salt Creek	1 – 87	c.1870	Warren	Owned by So Ohio Cov. Bridge Assoc.
NOBLE COUNTY							
5 Mi N W of Sarahsville			Buffalo Creek	1 – 49		Mult.Kingpost	
N of Mt Ephraim	Jesse Johnson		Opposum Run	1 – 40		Mult.Kingpost	
3½ Mi N of Summerfield	Gregg		Wills Creek	1 – 54		Mult.Kingpost	W/Aux. arch
2 Mi S of Olive Green	Manchester		Br of Olive Green Cr	1 – 49	1915	Mult.Kingpost	
2½ Mi S W of Sharon	Parrish		Olive Green Creek	1 – 78	1914	Mult.Kingpost	
5 Mi S of Sharon	Rich Valley		Olive Green Creek	1 – 65	1895	Mult.Kingpost	
3½ Mi N W of Middleburg	Gerst		Middle Fk Duck Cr	1 – 54		Mult.Kingpost	
2½ Mi N W of Dungannon			Keith Fork	1 – 66		Mult.Kingpost	
2½ Mi W of Honesty	Danford		Big Run	1 – 41		Mult.Kingpost	
5½ Mi S of Berne	Crumtown	A	East Fk Duck Cr	1 –		Kingpost	
1½ Mi S E of Middleburg	Wood Huffman		No Fk Duck Creek	1 – 57		Mult.Kingpost	
PERRY COUNTY							
1½ Mi S E of Chalfants	South		Br of Jonathan Creek	2 – 55		Mult.Kingpost	Slight hump
½ Mi S E of Chalfants	Church		Br of Jonathan Creek	1 – 55		Mult.Kingpost	Slight hump
East of Chalfants		AP	Br of Jonathan Creek	1 – 56		Mult.Kingpost	
3 Mi N E of Mt Perry			Kents Run	1 – 66		Mult.Kingpost	
3 Mi W of Somerset			Rush Creek	2 – 7l		Mult.Kingpost	Slight hump, orig. single span
PIKE COUNTY							
3 Mi N E of Waverly	Barger Farm	P	Old Bed of Ohio & Erie Canal	1 – 40		Kingpost	
PREBLE COUNTY							
4 Mi N of Fairhaven	Harshman		Four Mile Creek	1 – 109	1894	Childs	E. S. Sherman
3 Mi So of Eaton	Roberts		Seven Mile Creek	1 – 91	1829-30	Burr Double Lane	Orlistus Roberts & Joseph L.Campbell
1 Mi W of Gratis	Brubaker		Sams Run	1 – 88	1887	Childs	E. S. Sherman, to be moved.
3 Mi S W of New Westville	Lycurgus Beam		Elkhorn Creek	1 – 82	1887	Childs	E. S. Sherman
2 Mi N W of Eaton	Christman		Seven Mile Creek	1 – 100	1895	Childs	E.S. Sherman
3 Mi W of Lewisburg	Geeting		Price Creek	1 – 100	1894	Childs	E.S. Sherman
2 Mi N E of Lewisburg	Warnke		Swamp Creek	1 – 51	1895	Childs	E.S. Sherman
RICHLAND COUNTY							
1 Mi S of Rome			Black Fork Creek	1 – 115	1874	Smith	

LOCATION	NAME	OWNER	STREAM	Spans & Length	DATE	TYPE	BUILDER, etc.
ROSS COUNTY							
W of S Salem	Lower Twin Road		Buckskin Creek	1—100	1872	Smith	
SANDUSKY COUNTY							
4 Mi E of Burgoon	Mull Road		Wolf Creek	2— 99	1851-64	Town	Orig. single span
SCIOTO COUNTY							
3½ Mi S E of Minford	Bennett School		Lt. Scioto River	1—110	1867	Buckingham	
1 Mi. E of Minford	Kendall Road		Rocky Fork	1— 90		Kingpost	
S W of Otway			W Fk of Brush Creek	1—127	1874	Smith W/Aux. Arch	Smith Bridge Co.
SHELBY COUNTY							
2 Mi E of Lockington	Kirkwood Road		Great Miami River	1—168		Long	
SUMMIT COUNTY							
Everett			Furnace Run	1— 97	1877	Smith	
TRUMBULL COUNTY							
Newton Falls			E Branch Mahoning River	3—119		Town	Mr. Pinney-orig. single span, extra outside sidewalk
UNION COUNTY							
N E of N Lewisburg			Big Darby Creek	1— 95		Partridge	Reuben Partridge
N E of N Lesisburg	Spain Creek Road		Big Darby Creek	1— 72		Partridge	Reuben Partridge
N E of Irwin			Treacle Creek	1— 96		Partridge	Reuben Partridge
E of Irwin			Lt Darby Creek	1—112		Partridge	Reuben Partridge
3½ Mi S of Marysville			Big Darby Creek	1—154	c.1870	Partridge	Reuben Partridge
VINTON COUNTY							
1 Mi N E of Allensville	Mt. Oliver Road		Middle Branch Salt Cr.	1— 48	1875	Queenpost	G. W. Pilcher
1 Mi N of McArthur	Tinker			1— 62	1876	Kingpost Var.	Graves & Scott, moved to Fairground site 1967
4 Mi S W of Wilkesville	Geers Mill		Raccoon Creek	3—175	1874	Modified Burr Special Arch	Martin E. McGrath & Lyman Wells, floor has 19" chamber
Arbaugh	Mound Hill Road		Raccoon Creek	1—114	1871	Mult. Kingpost	Gilman & Ward Co. (slight hump)
4 Mi N of Creola	Cox		Brushy Fork	1— 40	1884	Queenpost	Jacob Diltz & Henry Steel
WASHINGTON COUNTY							
4 Mi W of Wolf Creek	Ransom Lane		W Br of Wolf Creek	1— 30		Mult.Kingpost	
1½ Mi N E of Patten Mills	Shinn		W Br of Wolf Creek	1—100	c.1886	Burr	
2 Mi N of Cutler	Henry		W Br of Lt Hocking Riv	1— 45	c.1892	Mult.Kingpost	
N of Decaturville	Root		W Br Lt Hocking Riv	1— 67	1888	Mult.Kingpost	
2 Mi N W of Watertown	Harra		S Br Wolf Creek	1— 95		Mult.Kingpost	
2 Mi N W of Barlow	Bell		S W Fork Wolf Creek	1— 63		Mult.Kingpost	
3 Mi N E of Barlow	Ormiston		Wolf Creek	1— 63		Mult.Kingpost	
Jackson Park Marietta	Schwenderman			1— 44		Mult.Kingpost	Moved from Churchtown 1967
3 Mi S W of Sitka	Hildreth		Lt Muskingum Riv	1—126		Howe	
Lawrence	Hune		Lt Muskingum Riv	1—123	c.1877	Buckingham	Rollin Meredith
2 Mi E of Wingett Run	Rinard		Lt Muskingum Riv	1—143	1874	Smith	
3 Mi S W of Yellow House	Baker		Leith Run	1— 45		Mult.Kingpost	
WYANDOT COUNTY							
5 Mi N E of Upper Sandusky	Parker		Sandusky River	1—161	1873	Howe	
2½ Mi S E of Nevada	Swartz		Sandusky River	1— 96	1880	Howe	

WISCONSIN

LOCATION	NAME	OWNER	STREAM	Spans & Length	DATE	TYPE	BUILDER, etc.
OZAUKEE COUNTY							
2 Mi N of Cedarburg			Cedar Creek	2—120	1876	Town	Orig. single span

Selected Bibliography

Bell, William E. *Carpentry Made Easy*. Philadelphia, 1857.

Cooper, Theodore. *American Railroad Bridges*. New York, (1889).

Duggan, George. *Specimens of the . . . Bridges . . . of . . . The United States Railroads*. New York, 1850.

Edwards, Llewellyn N. *A Record of History and Evolution of Early American Bridges*. Orono, Me., 1959.

Fletcher, Robert, and Snow, J. P. *A History of the Development of Wooden Bridges*. Paper No. 1864. American Society of Civil Engineers, New York, 1934.

Ketchum, Bryan E. *Covered Bridges on the Byways of Indiana*. Lockland, Ohio, 1949.

Kirby, Richard S., and Laurson, Philip G. *The Early Years of Modern Civil Engineering*. New Haven, 1932.

Long, Col. S. H. *Description of Col. Long's Bridges*. Concord, N. H., 1836.

Sellers, Charles Coleman. *Charles Willson Peale*. 1947.

Sloane, Eric. *American Barns and Covered Bridges*. New York, 1954.

Steinman, David B., and Watson, Sara Ruth. *Bridges and Their Builders*. New York, 1941.

Swanson, Leslie C. *Covered Bridges in Illinois, Iowa and Wisconsin*. Moline, Ill., 1960.

Town, Ithiel. *A Description of Ithiel Town's Improvement in the Principle, Construction and Practical Execution of Bridges*. New York, 1839.

Tyrrell, Henry G. *History of Bridge Engineering*. Chicago, 1911.

Wells, Rosalie. *Covered Bridges in America*. New York, 1931.

Also:

Buckeye Bridge Briefs. Northern Ohio Covered Bridge Society, 1959– ——.

Covered Bridge Chatter. Southern Ohio Covered Bridge Society, 1963– ——.

Covered Bridge Topics. National Society for the Preservation of Covered Bridges, Inc., 1942– ——.

CRVCBS Bulletin. Connecticut River Valley Covered Bridge Society, 1958– ——.

Indiana Covered Bridge Topics. Eugene R. Bock, Anderson, Inc., 1946–49.

Newsletter. Indiana Covered Bridge Society, 1964– ——.

Portals. Theodore Burr Covered Bridge Society of Pennsylvania, Inc., 1960– ——.

And:

World Guide to Covered Bridges. National Society for the Preservation of Covered Bridges, Inc., Boston, 1965.

Glossary

ABUTMENT—The shore foundation upon which a bridge rests, usually built of stone but sometimes of bedrock, wood, iron or concrete.

ARCH—A structural curved timber, or arrangement of timbers, to support a bridge, usually used in covered bridges together with a truss. Thus a *supplemental* or *auxiliary arch* is one which assists a truss and forms an arch-truss; a *true arch* bridge is entirely dependent upon the arch for support.

BENT—An arrangement of timbers resembling a saw-horse which is placed under a bridge at right angles to the stringers, sometimes used as a temporary scaffolding in building a covered bridge. Also to support light, open approaches, weak or damaged bridges, and sometimes as a substitute for abutments or piers.

BRACE—A diagonal timber in a truss which slants toward the midpoint of the bridge.

CHORD—The top (*upper chord*) or bottom (*lower chord*) member or members of a bridge truss, usually formed by the stringers; may be a single piece or a series of long joined pieces.

COMBINATION BRIDGE—Bridge designed for both highway and railroad traffic; also, a structure made with two types of trusses or combining features of two different trusses.

COMPRESSION MEMBER—A timber or other truss member which is subjected to squeeze. Often a diagonal member, such as a brace (q.v.) or counterbrace (q.v.).

CORBEL—In covered bridges, a solid piece of wood —mainly for decoration—which projects from the portal and assists in supporting the overhanging roof. Also, on a larger scale, a solid timber at the angle of an abutment (or pier) and lower chord to lend extra support.

COUNTERBRACE—A diagonal timber in a truss which slants away from the midpoint of the bridge (opposite from brace, q.v.).

DECK TRUSS—A type of bridge where the traffic, usually railroad, uses the roof on top of the truss as a roadbed; sometimes also carries traffic inside, between the trusses.

DOUBLE-BARRELED BRIDGE—Common designation for a covered bridge with two lanes; the divider can be a third truss or structural part of the bridge, or it can be a simple partition.

FACE OF ABUTMENT—The side of the abutment toward the center of the stream.

FALSEWORK—See SCAFFOLDING.

FLOOR BEAM—Transverse beam between bottom chords of trusses on which longitudinal joists are laid.

JOIST—Timbers laid longitudinally on the floor beams of a bridge and over which the floor planking is laid.

KEY—Piece, often a wedge, inserted in a joint such as a mortise-and-tenon to tighten the connection. Sometimes called a *fid*.

LAMINATED ARCH—A series of planks bolted together to form an arc; constructed in such a manner that the boards are staggered to give extra strength.

LATERAL BRACING—An arrangement of timbers between the two top chords or between the two bottom chords of bridge trusses to keep the trusses spaced apart correctly and to insure their strength. The arrangement may be very simple, or complex.

MORTISE, (n)—Cavity made in wood to receive a tenon. (v)—To join or fasten securely by using a mortise and tenon.

PANEL—Rectangular section of truss included between two vertical posts and the chords. A *panel system* is made up of three or more panels.

PARAPETS—Low masonry stone walls on either side of the section of roadway leading directly into a bridge. Common in Pennsylvania.

PATENTED TRUSS—Any one of the truss types for which United States patents have been granted, such as Burr, Town, Long, Howe, etc., trusses.

PIER—An intermediate foundation between abutments, built in the streambed, for additional support for the bridge. May be made of stone, concrete, wood, etc.

PILE—Heavy timber, often a peeled log, sunk vertically into the streambed to provide a foundation when the bottom is unreliable. Piling can be used as a base for abutments and piers, or the bridge can be built directly upon piling.

PORTAL—General term for the entrance or exit of a covered bridge; also used to refer to the boarded section of either end under the roof.

POST—Upright or vertical timber in a bridge truss; *centerpost* is the vertical timber in the center of a truss; *endpost* is the vertical timber at either end of the truss.

RAFTER—One of a series of relatively narrow beams joined with its opposite number to form an inverted V to support the roof boards of a bridge.

SCAFFOLDING—Light, temporary wooden platforms built to assist in the erection of a bridge. Sometimes called *falsework*.

SECONDARY CHORD—Single or joined timbers lying between upper and lower chords and parallel to them, giving added strength to the truss.

SHELTER PANEL—The first panel at each end of both trusses of a panel-truss bridge, often boarded on the inside to protect the timbers from moisture blowing through the portals.

SHIP'S KNEE—A short timber bent at a right angle used inside a covered bridge between a truss and upper lateral bracing to increase rigidity. Similar to a corbel (q.v.) but heavier and not decorative. Sometimes called *knee brace*.

SIMPLE TRUSS—An elementary bridge truss, such as kingpost or queenpost; not so large or complex as the patented trusses.

SKEW-BACK—A jog or incline in the face of an abutment to receive the end of a chord or an arch.

SKEWED BRIDGE—A bridge built diagonally across a stream.

SPAN—The length of a bridge between abutments or piers. *Clear span* is the distance across a bridge having no intermediate support, and measured from the face of one abutment to the face of the other. The length usually given is for the *truss span*, i.e., the length between one endpost of the truss and the other, regardless of how far the truss may overreach the actual abutment. Bridges of more than one span are called *multi-span bridges*.

SPLICE—A method of joining timbers, especially end-to-end, by means of a scarf or other joint, sometimes with keys or wedges inserted to give additional strength and stability to the joint. A *splice-clamp* is a metal or wooden clamp designed to hold two spliced timbers together.

STRINGER (or STRING-PIECE)—A longitudinal member of a truss which may be made up of either one single timber, in comparatively short bridges, or a series of timbers spliced end-to-end in longer bridges. Most evident in the chords (q.v.) which often go by this name.

SUSPENSION ROD (or HANGER ROD or SUSPENDER)—Iron rod usually found in arch bridges or in connection with auxiliary arches added to older bridges; attached from arch to floor beams to aid in supporting the roadway.

TENON—A tongue shaped at the end of a timber to fit into a mortise and so form a joint.

TENSION MEMBER—Any timber or rod of a truss which is subjected to pull, or stretch.

TIE-ROD—Iron rod used as integral vertical member in some truss bridges to replace wooden posts between upper and lower chords. Bridge members could be tightened by adjusting nuts against washers on the ends of the rods. Their use marked the first step in transition from wooden bridges to bridges made entirely of iron.

TREENAILS—Wooden pins which are driven into holes of slightly smaller diameter to pin members of lattice trusses together (pronounced "trunnels").

TRESTLE—A braced framework built up from the streambed to support a bridge.

THROUGH TRUSS—A covered bridge in which traffic uses a roadway laid on the lower chords between the trusses. Most covered bridges are through trusses.

TRUSS—An arrangement of members, such as timbers, rods, etc., in a rigid form so united that they support each other plus whatever weight is put upon the whole. Covered bridge trusses, including arch-trusses, employ a triangle or a series of combined triangles. *Truss* can designate just one side of a bridge, generally is used as meaning the combined sides.

TURNBUCKLE—A metal loop fashioned with a screw at one end and a swivel at the other, used in some covered bridge trusses to tighten iron rods and thus overcome sagging.

WEB—A truss design (such as Town lattice) in which timbers crisscross each other. A lattice truss, or a truss designed with overlapping panels, may be called a *web system*.

WEDGE—See KEY.

WINDBRACING—Inside timbers extending from a point on a truss to the ridgepole to attach the roof more firmly to the sides of the bridge.

Index

Notes on Bridges

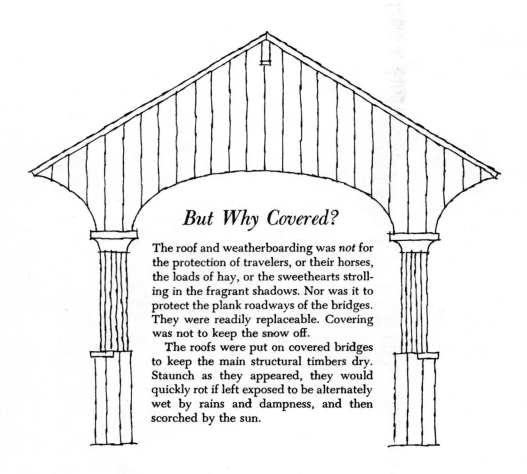

But Why Covered?

The roof and weatherboarding was *not* for the protection of travelers, or their horses, the loads of hay, or the sweethearts strolling in the fragrant shadows. Nor was it to protect the plank roadways of the bridges. They were readily replaceable. Covering was not to keep the snow off.

The roofs were put on covered bridges to keep the main structural timbers dry. Staunch as they appeared, they would quickly rot if left exposed to be alternately wet by rains and dampness, and then scorched by the sun.